Can You Trust the Media?

Can You Trust the Media?

Adrian Monck

with Mike Hanley

ICON BOOKS

This edition published in the UK in 2008 by
Icon Books Ltd, The Old Dairy, Brook Road,
Thriplow, Cambridge SG8 7RG
email: info@iconbooks.co.uk
www.iconbooks.co.uk

Sold in the UK, Europe, South Africa and Asia
by Faber & Faber Ltd, 3 Queen Square,
London WC1N 3AU
or their agents

Distributed in the UK, Europe, South Africa and Asia
by TBS Ltd, TBS Distribution Centre, Colchester Road
Frating Green, Colchester CO7 7DW

This edition published in Australia in 2008
by Allen & Unwin Pty Ltd, PO Box 8500,
83 Alexander Street, Crows Nest, NSW 2065

Distributed in Canada by
Penguin Books Canada, 90 Eglinton Avenue East,
Suite 700, Toronto, Ontario M4P 2YE

ISBN: 978-1840468-72-4

Typeset in 11.5pt Sabon by Wayzgoose

Printed and bound in the UK by Butler & Tanner

Contents

*To the friends and colleagues who
put themselves in harm's way.*

Adrian Monck is Professor of Journalism at City University
and an award-winning journalist who has worked with CBS
News, ITN and Sky News, and helped found Five News. He
was President of the Media Society 2005–6, and is also a
leading media blogger at adrianmonck.blogspot.com

Mike Hanley is a writer and journalist. He has written for
Reuters, *The Economist* and the *Financial Times*, and many
other titles.

Introduction

When Jeremy Paxman stood up to give his MacTaggart Lecture to the Edinburgh International Television Festival in 2007, he complained that Tony Blair had nicked his subject, just weeks before.

I know how he feels. First Blair, then Paxman. Is there anyone else out there who wants to pipe up on the subject of media trust? Are there any other exceedingly eminent people who want to 'reframe the debate'? Could any more public figures sift through recent media scandals, dredge up historical examples, expound eloquently and incisively on the subject of whether or not we can trust the media?

That, however, is the point. There is something really very important going on here. I don't think it is overstating the case to say that media trust is the biggest issue facing modern society. Think of an issue, any issue. Global warming. Democracy. Crime. Parenting. You name it, the media frames it. So, the media thing is the meta-issue that overhangs all the others. If you don't know whether or not you can trust the media, what the hell are you supposed to think about global warming? Hoax? Or not? Or what?

We *need* to trust the media. Or do we?

What I aim to do in this book is burst the trust balloon. I want to question just why it is we want to trust the media and lay out why that will never be possible. I'll look at how the media itself longs to be trusted and how it has carried on fighting for trust down the centuries. And last of all I want to look at how we can get by without trusting the

1

media to give us the information we need as citizens.

If that sounds straightforward, it's anything but. Because the media has become so all-encompassing, so embedded into our everyday existence, modern life is like a never-ending binge of junk food for the mind. Media trash crawls its way into every free part of your day: it is with you at home, in the car, on the train, at work and on holidays. Each day we swim through a modern soup of ones and noughts just to get to bed.

For an author, this is both an exhilarating and a terrifying subject. Exhilarating because every time you turn your computer on, there's a new angle: a kids' programme renaming a cat; a shark not (really) seen in Cornwall ... Terrifying because the half-life of a story, even the media story itself, is becoming increasingly close to zero. The media won't sit still for analysis long enough to give credibility to a blog post. Let alone a book.

Thing is, though, media trust is not just the topic of the hour. It's always the topic of the hour. From the Queen not storming out of a photo-shoot, back through Watergate, to the birth of the modern newspaper industry, to the first print runs of the Bible; how the media does what it does and why has rarely been a dull topic of discussion.

Meanwhile, the industry itself changes faster than Clark Kent in a phone booth. Certainly, anything written in book form about how media, the news, entertainment and all the rest is delivered will be out of date by the time the book hits the shelves. Expounding long theses on the impact of the RSS feed on newsgathering makes little sense when those engaged in the news trade either know what an RSS feed does for them, or are too busy to care.

So why is trust such an issue? As any tabloid editor will tell you, 'trust' is not important. Not being trusted never lost anyone a reader or a viewer. Editorial cock-ups and journalistic frauds are not followed by dramatic drops in circulation or ratings as hostile and suspicious audiences turn their backs. In fact, the evidence suggests that as long as we get the entertainment values right, audiences, and with them profits, will follow.

Of course, news broadcasts should be legal, decent, honest and truthful, but the same goes for TV ads. Asking whether you can 'trust' an advertisement is a pretty dumb question. Of course you can't, because the people behind them have an agenda – they want to sell you stuff. So do the people behind the news – they want you to watch or read, or text or whatever as long as you pay them … attention.

So how do we cope? I believe that instead of asking whether the media can be trusted, we need to teach people how to live in a world where trust is something that is withheld. People need to be sceptical as a matter of course. Then they won't be so disappointed. Scepticism is the faculty to which we should be appealing, but instead the media is tying itself in knots over credibility and trust.

▌▌ How to read this book ▌▌

What I've tried to do with this book is take the broadest look at the media that I can, extrapolating from small incidents in my life in journalism, applying some of the methodologies I learned when training as an historian and mixing in some of the analytical tools we use in journalism academia. What emerges is a picture of the media as an integral part of the way we live our lives and as an institution in its way every bit as crucial to our wellbeing as any other. Little wonder then that when it proves to be a fickle bearer of truth, we are struck with a bad case of the heebee jeebees.

The first two chapters look in detail at the recent crises in trust – the what, who, when, where and why of the events that have brought this issue to dominate so much of the public headspace – from the ethics of the editors of the *Sun* to the blatant fictions of the *New York Times* to the downfall of a generation of BBC bosses.

Chapter three looks at what I call the phenomenon of 'media bulimia', a compulsive modern pandemic caused by the viral reproduction of media into our awake time, and even our dreams. Where does it all come from, this media, and how do we live in the world it creates?

In chapter four, we look at the impact of the internet on trust. Can technology 'solve' trust? Or are we just getting new platforms that generate their own issues?

In chapter five, we examine that important sub-set of the media: the news. News is how we frame our world, it is the glasses we put on when we try to read our circumstances. It occupies a special place in our lives and always has. The question is, what do we want from our news? To understand that, we have to look at why it is produced the way it is, and from there we can ask how news is likely to change over the next few years.

Throughout history, the media has been accused of power-broking, of throwing its weight around in its own interests, of making and breaking our democracy. Well, maybe. In chapter six, I also look at the source of these rumours and think a bit about how true they might be.

Chapters seven and eight break the history of media trust into modern and ancient – modern history beginning with the birth of the American newspaper culture at the start of the twentieth century, and ancient with Gutenberg's invention of moveable type.

Conclusions are hard to come by in this morass, but there is one thing that I am convinced of and that is the more public information available, the better. In chapter nine, using recent terrorism cases along with examples from the world of business and their treatment by the media, I put forward my argument for a more transparent society. For me, transparency and information supersede our need for trust.

▌ What's trust got to do with it? ▐

Where does this trust obsession come from? The numbers show us that trust doesn't bring readers or viewers, but everyone from the Prime Minister down thinks it's important. Why?

In Britain, a media crisis is not a crisis until it engulfs the BBC, which dominates the media landscape like no other institution ever could and hopefully ever will. This current bout of media soul-searching, the endless round of debates and discussions, congealed around a series of BBC blunders – the Queen's trailers and a blatant fraud on the public with a premium-rate phone line among them. But the question is, why now? Journalists haven't changed the way they work – the public itself has always held the fourth estate in the contempt which it deserves. What has caused this current existential crisis?

For the BBC, it all started at the beginning of the 2000s. If you look back through old reviews from the 1980s and 1990s, you'll see BBC News described as 'authoritative'. But in the 21st century, 'authority' as a value has become seriously out of fashion. It implied distance and deference and it was difficult to measure. Our modern fixation with polling people and giving them what they want meant that the media industry no longer felt confident in its own judgements, instead handing leadership and content decisions over to a bunch of people who wouldn't know quality if it snuck up behind them and kicked their collective butts. The public, it turned out, thought it didn't want lectures from an authority figure; instead it wanted collegiality, phone-in polls, informality. It wanted to be able to 'trust' what it was being told, but it didn't want to have to do anything it didn't want to, like exercise its brain cells.

'Trust' looked like a good replacement for 'authority', and trust could be backed with numbers. Polls found that although people don't trust the media overall, they trusted some bits much more than others. Tabloids fared worst, followed by partisan 'quality' papers. Top of the trust heap were broadcasters. In a 2007 poll, broadcast journalists were considered twice as trustworthy as their local MP and three times as trustworthy as Tony Blair. Only 7 per cent of those polled thought that red-top reporters are trustworthy.

This trust data has been used to bolster the idea of media regulation. Broadcast journalists are highly regarded because they are highly regulated, runs the argument, not just because they have big audiences.

Ever since its establishment, British broadcasting had been governed by regulations that said its news had to show due impartiality and fairness.

Editors had achieved this principally by avoiding political controversy, or by adopting a seesaw, 'he said/she said' style of presentation, where every contentious point is matched by an uncontentious counter point. Faced with the divisive social issues of the 1970s and 1980s like Northern Irish terrorism and industrial disputes, television news did not take up arms on behalf of the proletariat, nor did it cheer-lead for the British Army in Ulster. Instead it mostly kept its distance, with what defenders viewed as studied neutrality and critics saw as an infuriating patrician hauteur.

By the 1990s this had gone on long enough to become a broadcast tradition. Few journalists swapped roles between newspapers and broadcasting. In the cosy duopoly of ITN and the BBC few even swapped companies. Even a new-comer like Sky News took so many of its journalists from ITN that it was known in the business as Sky-TN.

So when polls confirmed that broadcast news was 'trusted', this broadcast tradition and the regulation that underpinned it were saluted as avoiding the excesses of the press. Regulation delivered trust and trust was good.

Editors and executives adopted this argument both inside

and outside the BBC. As a broadcast news journalist and editor, I bought into it. But I was wrong. And if you want to know why, you have to go back to the place where the trust obsession began: the United States.

Back in the 1960s, in America, a strange shift took place. People began trusting the news from newspapers less and television more. How did this revolution in credibility occur?

The same period saw increased car ownership and commuting, the beginning of the evening news on TV and the decline of evening newspapers. People voted with their time and pollsters, commissioned by the broadcasters to flesh out the relationship between individuals and advertisers, were happy to discover that despite the novelty of TV news, viewers 'trusted' it. Trust meant that television – in case advertisers hadn't guessed already – was a great medium for selling. Of course, TV didn't need to prove itself. It was the sole route into the homes of millions of people and mass advertisers had to follow the people to sell their mass products.

What had newspapers done to lose favour and television to win it? Nothing.

The shift in trust reflected a shift in consumption. Quite simply, people trusted what they used, not vice versa. So firmly was that shift imprinted on public opinion that in the years following his retirement from presenting CBS News, anchor Walter Cronkite was still rated as the most trusted man in America.

Cronkite is still with us, but he is no longer as trusted. He hasn't been caught shoplifting or dodging taxes, but a couple of decades' absence from the nightly screens of Americans has eroded his trustworthiness. Cronkite has not been alone in experiencing this coastal erosion. TV might have overtaken newspapers in trust ratings but Americans' confidence in public institutions as a whole began to crumble as the twentieth century matured.

One of the best analyses of that shift is by two American

academics, Paul Gronke and the late Timothy Cook. They looked back at years of polling data and concluded that these were the main attributes of people who said they trusted the media:

- Young
- Badly educated
- Poor
- Non-churchgoers
- Democrat
- Non-partisan

What made people distrust the media? Just switch it around to any one of these characteristics:

- Older
- University educated
- Wealthy
- Socially conservative
- Republican
- Highly partisan

And those attributes read something like the headline social and demographic changes in the United States in the past quarter of a century: Ageing baby boomers. Better education. Higher pay. Republicans enjoying long spells controlling the White House and Congress. The rise of the religious right and strengthened conservative values. These trends increased the numbers of people likely to distrust the media. The sole demographic factor in the media's favour was a drop in church attendance.

Americans who were older, smarter and better off were more sceptical of the news media, but they remained its most devoted audience.

▌ What makes us trust? ▐

[T]elevision provides a new (or, possibly, restores an old) definition of truth: the credibility of the teller is the ultimate test
of the truth of a proposition. 'Credibility' here does not refer
to the past record of the teller for making statements that have
survived the rigours of reality testing. It refers only to the
impression of sincerity, authenticity, vulnerability or attractiveness ...

Neil Postman

What makes us trusting? The answer to this question is in
two parts. Firstly, who we are as people makes us more or
less sceptical, more or less trusting, more or less gullible.
Secondly, the way the news is presented, in print and on the
box, increases and decreases its perceived trustworthiness.

The one salient truth in the whole trust quagmire is that
your level of 'trustingness' – gullibility perhaps – is determined by who you are. Your age, sex, income, education,
geography, media use patterns and your point of view
regarding specific issues are all crucial determinants of how
sceptical or trusting you are of the information fed to you
by the media.

According to reams of evidence from academic studies,
mostly undertaken in the United States, the two factors that
best predict what you will think of the news are money and
education. Wealthy, well-educated types are generally media
sceptics, as Gronke and Cook concluded. What is interesting here is that, since the end of the Second World War, as
rich societies have undergone a golden age of almost uninterrupted economic growth, we have all become richer
and generally better educated. We have, in effect, created a
society of sceptics.

Other predictors of scepticism? Metropolitan types are
more sceptical. Again, more of us than ever before live in
cities and this too has contributed to the sceptical society.

9

Age is slightly more variable. Eighteen- to 24-year-olds are more trusting of the media, the over-45s less so and 25- to 44-year-olds least of all. But in the post-baby boom era, the middle-aged outnumber the young. Indeed, the social forces driving scepticism are in the ascendant.

However, there are psychological factors at work too.

Decades-worth of studies have shown that television generally scores higher on credibility than newspapers. This trend first shows up in American surveys at the beginning of the 1960s, when television news was still relatively new. The findings have held up pretty well over the years, although inconsistencies and variations have emerged when specific aspects of credibility are looked at, and also when audiences are broken down by where they live and by their social and political views.

So, why is it that television news is seen to be more credible than news in print? Visual realism is the most obvious explanation. 'I'll believe it when I see it' isn't a well-known saying for nothing. People are simply more inclined to believe what they can see. The processing priority we give to visual information gives moving images a head start in the credibility stakes. Television producers know this instinctively – there is no news without pictures. The first serious current affairs programme on American television was called simply, *See It Now*.

Another credibility booster for the box is what's called 'affective appeal', otherwise known as the good-looking newscaster. Television news has a high population of attractive people among reporters and newscasters, and attractive people are more persuasive. Perhaps, but by that token Fox News, with its parade of attractive anchors, ought to be a beacon of fair and balanced reportage, a fact not lost on fake newscaster Jon Stewart's *The Daily Show*. 'How the news is presented, packaged if you will, is also an important part of the sales pitch. Yes, attractiveness matters,' says

Stewart, followed by a piece presented by comedian Samantha Bee entitled 'NILF – News I'd Like to F@#K'. Among Samantha's gags:

> Jennifer Eccleston's screen says Baghdad but her open neckline says 'Bag These'.

> And Kiran Chetry interviews someone just back from Iraq in a skirt that barely covers her Sunni triangle.

The Daily Show aside, physical appearance does matter. It affects credibility. Or at least the absence of physical attractiveness undermines it.

What else do we know about television news and credibility? If you read the news fluently (but not too fluently), you're more credible and if you're pleasant, you're more likely to be thought competent.

All of which adds up to a reminder that superficiality remains an important part of credibility in front of the camera, whatever the platform. But polls and personalities aren't the whole story. They're only the beginning of the modern trust crisis in journalism.

And this is what the British media has come to value above all else? Years of measuring trust have generated a voluminous amount of poll data. Academics have analysed the people who have it and those that don't – what builds the numbers and what erodes them. Everything, in short, but actual truth, credibility and professionalism.

There are important issues about the way the media conducts itself, but they're not important because we need to build 'trust'. Trust is a shoddy yardstick. It doesn't gauge truth, it gauges what looks close to the truth: verisimilitude – not a word to use after a late night out.

As journalists, we tend to sneer at intellectualism and value pragmatism. If broadcasters are going to take their editorial policies seriously, then they need to get over the current obsession with 'trust' and engage with the moral contradictions and intellectual problems at the heart of those policies. And that might require a little more philosophy and a little less marketing.

CHAPTER ONE

Trust Me, I'm a Journalist

After the British National Party (BNP) had scored one of their modest local election victories, I invited its party spokesman – a fascist and anti-Semite – to appear live on a news programme I ran. Although we could have interviewed him in the main newsroom, I arranged for him to be put in a remote studio somewhere else in London.

When he'd installed himself, and just before the interview began, I had his microphone muted while the presenter read out his previous convictions (beating up a Jewish schoolteacher was just one of them), as they ran on a little graphic beneath him. This before giving him the chance to respond.

I didn't tell him I was going to do it before he came on. I had stitched him up and he wasn't happy.

How could I justify that? After all, people voted for the BNP and either they did it hoping that a vote for the party would send a message, or because they sympathised with its nudge-nudge, wink-wink neo-Nazism. My personal crusade was to let those voters know about the kind of people they had endorsed through the ballot box.

As background, I had previously been on the end of a BNP-orchestrated email campaign for previous crimes against god-fearing white folk. My favourite term of abuse was 'nigger-loving Jew' – a self-incriminating double whammy from a supporter of a party which claims to have left racism and anti-Semitism behind.

So you could say this was just a chance to get even. Alternatively it was a way of drumming up some cheap controversy on a slow news night.

But, if I said I did it in the public interest – my very own perverse version of the public interest – you'd just have to trust me. My point? Trust is fundamentally a personal attribute – it belongs to people.

Not that we don't plaster the word around. Although we inhabit a complex world, we still like to use simple ideas drawn from personal relationships, like trust, to talk about our altogether more complicated relationships with impersonal things, like corporations and governments, religion and money.

For the past half-century or so, the way the people who run those institutions have tried to make sense of those relationships is by putting numbers to them. It's how retailers have judged the effectiveness of their advertising and politicians their performance outside of election campaigns.

Polls generate numbers and numbers are solid. But when the concepts they measure are as vague as trust, those numbers don't always help. Don't take my word for it: when philosopher Onora O'Neill addressed the issue of trust – in all institutions – in the BBC's Reith Lectures in 2002, she pointed out another problem:

> How good is the evidence for this crisis of trust? A lot of the most systematic evidence for the UK can be found in public opinion polls and similar academic research. The pollsters ask carefully controlled cross-sections of the public whether they trust certain professions or office-holders ... In answering the pollsters we suppress the complexity of our real judgements, smooth out the careful distinctions we draw between different individuals and institutions, and average our judgements about their trustworthiness in different activities.

So why has trust become so important for the media? What I chronicle in this book is the story of an obsession with trust. And there are many parts to this mania.

On the most basic level it stems from issues of trust that are personal, or 'affective'. This is the trust that begins with people living together in cities, forced to find ways of dealing with one another, encountering strategies for deception, and attempting to counter them. It takes us back to the Greek city-states and Socrates, and it remains a constant theme, translated from a meeting on the street to an audio-visual encounter. The way people look, the things they say – these things remain important.

On the next, it is the story of a transfer of faith from a media based purely around religion to a media based on news. That transfer left parts of the media with a peculiar sense of their own mission, the inheritors of the preaching and moralising that had once been directed from the pulpit and the platform.

And lastly it is a story of all those things that we assume add up to trust but really don't, and how a media that lost readers and viewers began to regard its failure not in market terms but in moral ones.

Decline in readers and viewers was seen by the media as a symptom not of changing demographics or lifestyles but of a loss of trust. Salvation lay in somehow recapturing it. So trust became a grail to be searched for.

But why? What's important is not whether the BBC, as an organisation, is trusted but whether the information that comes out of the BBC is reliable. We care about whether or not the BBC is telling the 'truth'. The problem comes, of course, because the media is part of the reality that creates that 'truth'. It's a kind of never-ending Escher puzzle, with media executives and the public wandering inside it, trying to end up on the same level.

To complicate all this, over the last decade we've been

confronted by this whole new audience-becoming-the-media conundrum, with the blogosphere mushrooming in direct proportion to the amount of fertiliser it creates. Google, as a news aggregator, brings together more news in a day than the BBC generates in a year.

Wikipedia, with its almost instant updating, could well turn out to be the most wonderfully reliable news resource the world has ever seen. But, then again, it might not. If you want to know whether or not to trust it, there is only one way – find out how it works. 'Wiki', in new media parlance, stands for 'what I know is'. Well, what I know is that Wikipedia, as with the rest of the blogosphere, is an open-source collaboration: some contributors don't know what they are talking about, others are just plain mischievous, and good information is mixed up with bad in a way that's hard to unpick.

Our ability to 'trust' the media is, in other words, directly proportional to how much we understand it: what it is, why it is and how it works.

▮▮ Great white lies ▮▮

First things first: what do journalists themselves think about the trust thing? Do they care whether or not their readers trust them? Do the editors of tabloids like Britain's *Sun* or America's *New York Post* stay awake at night worrying about whether or not their journalism is trusted? Yeah, right. They may stay awake wondering whether more people will pick up their newspaper tomorrow than did so today. They may stay awake wondering if the phone will ring with an incandescent Rupert on the end furious about the editorial line. But do they care if you trust them?

Much of the time, the answer to that question seems to be emphatically 'no'. Despite the fact checking, the editorial processes and the elaborate constructs put in place by parts of the media to ensure that 'standards' are met, we are constantly being let down by our news professionals. There are countless examples and they arise every day. Why?

The simplest answer is money. From a commercial perspective, trust is a worthless asset for media owners.

Sceptical? Here is one example that shows in the most brutal way that media owners are actually rewarded by breaching their readers' trust.

In the summer of 2007 the *Sun* reported:

> Shocked tourists told of their terror last night over the Great White shark sighting off Cornwall. And one holidaymaker said: 'This has got to be every swimmer's worst nightmare.'
>
> The Jaws alert was raised after stunned dad Nick Fletcher filmed the fearsome fish just 200 yards from a beach in St Ives. He was videoing dolphins and only realised the killer shark was hunting among them when he watched the footage at home. Last night Britain's leading shark expert Richard Peirce confirmed the 12ft creature was definitely a predatory shark and there was every chance it was a Great White – immortalised in the 1975 Steven Spielberg movie *Jaws*.
>
> Excited Richard, chairman of the Shark Trust, spoke out after studying Nick's astonishing film. He said: 'It clearly has a white belly like a Great White. And something about the way it breaches – twisting as it leaps out of the water – also suggests it is.'

Peirce posted a rather less 'excited' comment on the Shark Trust's website:

> Richard's opinion was that it was impossible to make a conclusive identification, and that the shark could either have been a mako, a porbeagle, or, if one accepts that white sharks are occasional vagrant visitors in UK waters, these animals could not be ruled out.

Still, a couple of days later, the *Sun* had another shark story:

> Horrified mum Catherine Price videoed a 'harmless' shark off
> Cornwall – then discovered it was Britain's JAWS.
>
> Holidaymaker Catherine was on a boat trip with son
> Callum, seven, when they spotted the 12ft monster's fin.
>
> As it circled in the water, fellow tourists dismissed the crea-
> ture as a docile basking shark.
>
> But Catherine got the shock of her life yesterday – as
> experts confirmed it could well be the second sighting of a
> deadly GREAT WHITE prowling off St Ives.

The *Guardian* followed up the story by interviewing an expert:

> David Sims, who leads the only scientific study of large sharks
> in the UK, at the Marine Biological Association in Plymouth,
> said: 'The *Sun* seems to run this story every summer. Just
> because parliament has gone into recess does not make this a
> Great White shark.'

Sims concluded that the first video claiming to show a shark
actually showed a pod of dolphins or porpoises and a more
recent one featured a basking shark, a distinctly non-
aggressive creature that eats only plankton:

> Those clips provide no evidence that there is a Great White
> shark. We have been studying sharks for twelve years and in
> all that time we have never seen a Great White. With the fre-
> quency that tourists supposedly spot them, you might think
> we would have seen one by now.

Dr Sims' remarks didn't make it into the *Sun*. But the next
day they had something better, the *pièce de résistance*:

> Great White shark fever gripped the West Country last night –
> amid claims that *another* of the man-eaters has been sighted.
>
> A Cornish newspaper printed a dramatic photo of what is

said to be one of the beasts just a mile off the popular resort of Newquay.

The snap was taken by amateur angler Kevin Keeble, who was fishing for mackerel when he spotted a dorsal fin about 100ft from his hired boat.

Alas, Kevin's photo was taken not off the coast of Cornwall, but Cape Town in South Africa. Other papers reported the 'great white lie'. The *Sun* didn't bother to tell its readers. It might have spoilt things for them. Instead, they ran a DVD giveaway of *Jaws* and continued with the shark stories.

The price paid by the *Sun* for peddling such nonsense? According to the circulation figures, a modest spike in sales. It was, after all, the silly season. So had readers already discounted the *Sun*'s credibility? Are half-truths just what we expect from a tabloid? Is the *Sun*'s editor lying sleepless in London? Not over that little prank.

Today, with focus groups and market research, news executives have a better understanding of the social composition and attitudes of consumers than at any time since printers with ink on their fingers were able to greet their customers by name. No significant research conclusively links drops in readership (or listening or viewing) to specific issues of credibility. In other words, shark stories carry no financial penalty. In fact, readers reward them.

Claims of distrust, unfairness and downright deceit echo down the ages and many remedies have been proposed. But there is little evidence to suggest that proprietors or editors would be willing to make the kinds of changes that critics claim would make the news media more credible to the public. And why should they?

In a way, though, the shark story and the amount of 'trust' press it got, was a shaggy dog. The *Sun* 'lies': STOP THE PRESSES! Hardly. Everyone knows the tabloids are full of shit. According to polls, less than 10 per cent of the British public thinks red top journalists are trustworthy. But it doesn't really matter. If we know it's a rag that is published for the profit of its proprietor and as a distraction for the nation's population of plumbers and shopkeepers, tearing our hair out over every lie and sensation is an unproductive waste of time.

More important, and at the heart of the trust debate, is what has happened in recent years at the quality end of the market – in particular to the BBC and to the most trusted of our media professionals, broadcasters. This has been the real source of the industry wailing and breast-beating.

In 2007, a series of scandals broke out across the British media like pimples on an adolescent face. From the great white lies at the *Sun* through to the highest echelon of the British establishment – the BBC – it seemed that nothing the media did could be trusted.

What caused all this? In short, the root of all evil: money.

It's not that journalists are more corrupt or lazy now than they have ever been. More that the traditional regulators of media trust – structures, regulations, codes of conduct – have been broken down in recent years as the media industry entered the 21st century lean and mean. Mistakes, oversights and downright deception have become rife.

▮▌ Cooking up trouble ▐▮

Although the BBC is publicly funded, commercial broad-casters are reliant on advertising cash. To increase profit-ability, in recent years they rolled up their sleeves and got to work reducing programme budgets and looking for new revenue streams. They found it in competitions: text votes and premium-rate phone lines.

These allow them to make money not just from the space between programmes, but also from the programmes them-selves.

In 2001, *Big Brother* alone netted over £4 million from 16 million text and premium-rate phone line votes. 'Audience participation' in the form of voting has been a goldmine for broadcasters and the ruse has spread from annual event shows, like *I'm A Celebrity ... Get Me Out Of Here!* to morning TV issues votes, late-night sex phone-in votes and everything in between.

But the whole edifice began to crumble thanks to a bit of cross-platform joining of the dots. What do I mean? Well, one weekend a sharp-minded radio listener who turned his TV on, went online to post a comment on a forum. This is what he wrote:

> I'm being a bit dense here, (I'm not long up) but *Saturday Kitchen* invites people to phone in with their questions, so I assumed it was live. Radio 5 Live also encourages people to phone/text so I thought that was live. Eamonn Holmes is on both programmes this morning – which one is live?

Turns out the TV phone vote was indeed a con. Others swapped similar stories. Newspapers picked up on it. As it dawned on people that television competitions might not be as trustworthy as they'd assumed, still more examples were examined and found to be bogus. The BBC itself was found to be one of the most flagrant phone poll fraudsters: among the fraudulent results were the winners of Comic Relief 2007; *TMi* in September 2006; Sport Relief, July 2006; Children In Need, November 2005 ... the list went on. Clearly, the BBC as well as other broadcasters had adopted a new way of doing business – fraud – and taken to it like a duck to water. Not a good look.

Then came a trivial mistake, but one that almost brought the BBC to its knees and shows the damage that the fragmentation of the broadcasting industry has done to the things that protect the public's trust.

▮▮ The creation of conflict ▮▮

Under a directive called 'Television Without Frontiers', the European Commission requires broadcasters to set aside 10 per cent of their programmes for independent productions. That quota is set to rise when a new directive – 'Audiovisual Media Services' – supersedes it. The idea is to encourage diversity and break up old state monopolies.

But Britain was way ahead of Brussels, thanks to the 2003 Communication Act. That piece of legislation required the BBC to spend about half its programme budgets across all channels with independent producers – in 2006 that ran to about £350 million.

In the early 1980s, these 'indies' had been a rather charming cottage industry of jobbing broadcasters and former executives. But the BBC didn't like dealing with lots of little people. It came up with a list of preferred suppliers (you guessed it, bigger companies) and the market whittled numbers down to a few large indies – companies like RDF, Endemol, Shine and Talkback Thames.

The big indies were lean and mean. They didn't carry headcount, instead they relied on freelancers to staff programmes by contract. Nor did they worry unduly about training and compliance. They were in business to make money, but that was hard because the people who commissioned content from them – the BBC in the main – wanted to cut costs.

As the success of 'reality' television grew with the arrival of shows like *Wife Swap* and *Faking It*, commissioners increasingly wanted to standardise stories. There was nothing new in that. Tabloid newspapers had done the same thing for years. One *New York Post* editor – a Brit, of course – would famously wander round his newsroom asking for a 'baby story'. Reality TV stories had to be made to conform to 'bibles'. Formats required a certain amount of confrontation but they also demanded collaboration from 'real' people.

To give you an example, friends of ours wangled a slot on a property programme. The show had an agreeable host who advised would-be property developers. The format was simple – forget people successfully taking some gentle advice, instead create dramatic tension between the expert host and the ingénue developer.

To create that tension, shopping trips were arranged to look at expensive products to suggest that my friends had material aspirations that would 'break' their budget. The host was suitably embarrassed about the need to 'stunt up' confrontations. The production team was friendly and apologetic.

The programme ended with a reckoning of how costly the project had been. All improvements were costed at list price. But my pals had negotiated price reductions and free-bies based on their use of the products in the TV pro-gramme (the producers kindly passed on some numbers), so although the programme showed a loss, in actual fact they paid a fraction of the real price.

It didn't end there. Estate agents were asked to conjure up valuation figures (against all their professional codes) and were the people who came round at the end really buy-ers? Still, my friends were happy to phoney up an ending where they admitted losing money, because actually they hadn't.

They were bought and sold for a fitted kitchen, happily complicit in the whole charade. Yes, you would probably say it's harmless enough stuff – consenting adults, nobody died. Maybe. I say that you can wipe clean a granite top but not the chrome-plated handle of your conscience. And it's a slippery slope.

In this case it may all have been pretty harmless, but there were many victims of 'reality' who didn't walk away with a new en suite bathroom. New technology has given them the opportunity to answer back, quickly and publicly.

The online media that opened up email, forums and blogs gave people who felt they'd had an unfair crack of the whip an opportunity to set the record straight. It also let TV viewers compare notes. Dangerous stuff.

∎ Auntie and Her Majesty ∎

In the late 1990s, BBC producer Stephen Lambert quit the BBC for an independent production company, RDF. At the Beeb, Lambert had run a highbrow documentary strand called *Modern Times*, which featured individual films. RDF wanted to use those skills, but not for esoteric one-offs. They wanted formats that could be traded at international TV fairs. Lambert helped oversee successful reality shows like *Wife Swap*, where women traded partners and families, and *Faking It*, which trained novices to see if they could fool a panel of professionals. The shows were all about conflict.

Lambert had been encouraged to join RDF by taking a slice of the company's equity and he was well rewarded. RDF was a success. It won a lot of business with Channel 4 and it sold many shows around the world. It gobbled up UK rivals, among them Scotland's biggest production company, Wark Clements. When RDF listed in 2005, it was valued at £50 million. By 2007, that valuation had almost doubled and Lambert had the title Chief Creative Officer.

But then the company ran into trouble from an entirely unexpected quarter. When Peter Fincham, the controller of BBC1, held a press launch to announce the autumn programme line-up, one of the jewels in his schedule was an RDF series, *A Year With The Queen*. The programme was a bargain, since the BBC put up only half the cash – RDF would be expected to find the rest selling it overseas.

Unlike the forced confrontations of RDF's regular programming, this was a simple fly-on-the-wall exercise, filmed and directed by one person. What could go wrong?

Peter Fincham showed journalists a trailer for the pro-gramme. He didn't know it, but it had been cut by RDF's Stephen Lambert as a sales pitch for international clients. A brief voice-over promised a behind-the-scenes look at the Royals and a bunch of clips were cut together, obviously out of sequence.

One clip was a brief verbal exchange between celebrity photographer Annie Leibovitz and the Queen. It was fol-lowed by a clip of the Queen walking down a corridor com-plaining about getting dressed up. Fincham introduced it like this: 'Annie Leibovitz gets it slightly wrong and the Queen walks out in a huff.'

Had he said nothing, the editing could have been dis-missed as simply misleading. But that simple sentence mis-represented the sequence.

Clutching their DVDs, reporters rushed back to break the story of the royal 'strop'. Never mind that in an inter-view in May, Leibovitz had mentioned that the Queen wasn't happy about wearing heavy robes, but had been good-humoured. The pictures of the Queen walking off 'in a huff' were in fact of her arriving. The exchange with Leibovitz was so brief it was impossible to tell if she was kidding around or admonishing. And in fact on the rushes, she chuckled immediately afterwards.

The next day, at lunchtime, the BBC was forced to issue a public apology. None of the journalists concerned felt the need to apologise for their failures to check the story.

Two brief shots and a few words ended up creating a big-ger corporate crisis than the entire Hutton enquiry into the veracity of reporting over the Iraq war (more of which in chapter two). There was a difference too. Whereas Hutton was a political dispute that had generated considerable pub-lic sympathy, this was a simple case of misrepresentation for the purposes of entertainment.

RDF kept publicly silent about its role in it. Meanwhile,

the BBC and ITV – who provided a fifth of the company's business – both announced they would put commissions on hold. A week later Lambert was buying thousands of pounds worth of shares in his own company to help prop up its sinking share price. He also admitted to editing the trailer:

> In retrospect, this was a serious editorial misjudgement, but in this context, and without any commentary, these shots did not convey the interpretation that was later placed on them as being a record of the Queen storming out. All that was being attempted was to convey a brief sense of a slightly ruffled encounter.

'It's only now with the share price in freefall that it is appropriate to set the record straight because it is no longer about RDF's relationship with the BBC but investor confidence in the company,' Chief Executive David Frank told one newspaper.

As expressions of remorse go for damaging the public service traditions of the BBC by sensationalising an encounter with the Queen, it wasn't too convincing. Lambert's own admission had been prompted by a desire to prop up RDF's share price. He had at least offered his resignation. Frank refused to accept it.

Frank told journalists: 'The public don't give a damn about independent production companies and how they're financed or structured. They care about what's on TV. They don't give a damn about who RDF is.'

Nobody came out of this little drama with honour. The journalists who had reported the 'huff' could have checked their own cuttings. The *Sun* had headlined the story 'Throne A Wobbler'. But back in May, it had reported:

> Ms Leibovitz, who has photographed a host of Hollywood celebrities, said she was 'honoured' to take the atmospheric snaps at Buckingham Palace.

But [she] admitted the Queen was not the easiest subject at first when she was called to wear some of her Royal robes for the shoot.

The *Vanity Fair* photographer said the Queen entered the room and muttered: 'Why am I wearing these heavy robes in the middle of the day?'

'She doesn't really want to get dressed up anymore. She just couldn't be bothered.

'I admire her for that. When you get to that age, you have a right to have those kinds of feelings.'

The newspapers that fed the story couldn't even trust their own reporting. Eventually both Fincham and Lambert resigned. But as they clung on, an even deeper crisis was brewing.

▐ Death watch ▐

The crisis wasn't just triggered by commercial pressure and a desire by other media to catch broadcasters out. Although reality TV had originally grown out of 'observational' experiments by social scientists, the chief proponents of reality TV had never spent long grappling with the ethics of the genre. Paul Watson had brought Britain its first fly-on-the-wall series in 1974 with a twelve-part account of a Reading family, the Wilkins. Its generic title, *The Family*, was as much a social and political statement as the films themselves.

In the 1980s, Watson went to Australia and skewered wealthy suburban life through a portrayal of a dysfunctional dynasty in *Sylvania Waters*. It was a huge hit, a real-life soap opera to compete with another fictional hit of the time, *Dallas*.

Even then, the unlovable bunch at the centre of the films pleaded that they had been misrepresented. But television, rationed to a handful of channels, was in the ascendant.

Ratings in their millions provided a scornful rebuff to critics, even when those critics were the subjects themselves.

Watson was frank about his methods, happy to play the part of puppet master. Back in the mid-nineties, he gave this account of himself:

> People accuse me of manipulation and I admit to manipulation – in the cutting-room. It's called editing. If you shoot ten shots, what do you do? You exercise prejudice, passion, certain proclivities. You build up an authored view ...
>
> I'm a devious, subversive, difficult sod of a film-maker, because now I know my craft skills so well I can make people five days later feel the hidden agenda to a film. Hidden agenda sounds so Machiavellian, but it isn't.

But times changed. In 2007, he produced a more sober film about a man dying of Alzheimer's. Despite its rather maudlin title, *Malcolm and Barbara: Love's Farewell*, the film dealt intelligently with Barbara Pointon caring for her dying husband.

Publicity for the film claimed that the documentary 'ends when Barbara calls Paul to ask him to come as Malcolm is about to die ... In moving scenes, Malcolm is surrounded by his family and Barbara strokes his head as he passes away.'

At a press screening, the *Guardian* reported that journalists 'were left with the impression that the scene ended with the filming of his moment of death, as the shot froze on Mr Pointon's still face.'

Mrs Pointon spoke movingly of her husband's death. She told the Daily *Mail*:

> I'm sure I will be pilloried for allowing his death to be shown ... but it had to be done ... We went into it wanting to raise awareness of this awful disease. He would have said, 'What is the point of sanitising things? Let's tell the whole story', which is how it should be.

How did this come to light? Well, a columnist's moralising on the awfulness of death and the shamefulness of reality television led to Mrs Pointon's brother-in-law Graham writing to set her straight:

> In the new film, we see my brother, Malcolm Pointon, dying. We do not see him die – filming finished three days before Malcolm stopped breathing, so the argument about the ethics of showing this on television, while important, does not apply to this case. I was there on the Monday before Malcolm's death, and heard Paul say, as he left, that he had enough material for the film, and would now leave the family in peace. He did not return that week. Malcolm died on the following Thursday morning.

Watson's camera had captured Malcolm Pointon's final moments of consciousness, not life, and a semantic argument ensued that meant his passing became grist to the mill of the media debate, expressing not the family tragedy it undoubtedly was, but the tragedy of journalism and TV fakery.

There is a problem all right. But it's not exclusive to television, to our times, or to this country.

▌ Little Jimmy ▐

Ron comes back into the living room, syringe in hand, and calls the little boy over to his chair: 'Let me see your arm.'

He grabs Jimmy's left arm just above the elbow, his massive hand tightly encircling the child's small limb. The needle slides into the boy's soft skin like a straw pushed into the centre of a freshly baked cake. Liquid ebbs out of the syringe, replaced by bright red blood. The blood is then re-injected into the child.

Jimmy was just eight when that story appeared in a Sunday edition of the *Washington Post*, in September 1980. The next year, it won for its reporter Janet Cooke, a young, ambitious woman in her mid-twenties, the highest accolade in American journalism – a Pulitzer Prize.

The *Washington Post*, local newspaper to the most powerful government on earth, was already legendary for its journalism. Two of its reporters, Bob Woodward and Carl Bernstein, had played a key role in uncovering the Watergate scandal that had ended the presidency of Richard Nixon.

In America, Watergate was the mountain from which public trust in the media came down. The story of a corrupt president exposed by two plucky reporters from the *Washington Post* boosted people's faith in the fourth estate. In the weeks that followed Richard Nixon's departure from office, opinion polls put 'trust and confidence' in the news media at nearly 70 per cent.

That trust was won against the odds: the *Washington Post* had been virtually alone in committing resources to the story of the Watergate break-in. Media competitors accused the paper of hyping the story.

Before Watergate, journalists had been held in the public's contempt. The feature film of the Watergate story, *All the President's Men*, probably expressed the public's opinion of journalists best.

'You people,' one interviewee says to Robert Redford and Dustin Hoffman, 'you think you can come into my home, ask a few questions, have me destroy the reputations of men that I work for and respect. Do you understand loyalty? Have you ever heard of loyalty?'

The post-Watergate boost was short-lived. By the time the story of 'Little Jimmy' was published, journalists were right down there in the public's consciousness with ambulance-chasing lawyers and politicians again.

And Janet Cooke's tale of a child heroin addict in a black ghetto shooting up in front of a reporter did not restore the public's faith in the fourth estate. It aroused outrage and hostility in equal measure. The *Washington Post*'s phone lines lit up with complaints. Although Cooke was black, the story was labelled racist and the paper's apparent lack of concern for the fate of the child, criminal.

Washington's mayor was incandescent. Local police launched a mammoth citywide search. Teachers, social workers – anyone who might know anything was asked for information on Jimmy. Cooke's story was syndicated to hundreds of other newspapers across America and around the world.

The *Post* refused to reveal either Jimmy's identity or his whereabouts. But the journalistic defence of anonymity rang a little hollow in the face of a child in grave peril. The authorities threatened Janet Cooke with a court order to get the information. But they never got it, because Jimmy didn't exist and his story was fiction.

It wasn't the lies in the story that found Cooke out. Her piece had gone through an editorial chain of command that included Bob Woodward, of Watergate fame, and his boss, executive editor Ben Bradlee. Colleagues who had been suspicious of the headline-grabbing piece were branded 'jealous'.

The paper's fact-checking capabilities let Ms Cooke slide on by. In the end, she was tripped up by the competition: a significant *Private Eye* moment, perhaps, or a case of the media holding its own to account.

When reporters from the Associated Press called the colleges she'd listed on her CV to get their reaction to a star student's success, they discovered she wasn't telling the truth about her university education. The details that had gone forward with her prize application were lies. Confronted over her personal history, she was also questioned hard over the Jimmy story and the truth did out.

She had to return her Pulitzer.

Ben Bradlee, the *Washington Post*'s chief, exculpated himself like this:

The credibility of a newspaper is its most precious asset, and it depends almost entirely on the integrity of its reporters. When that integrity is questioned and found wanting, the wounds are grievous, and there is nothing to do but come clean with our readers, apologize ... and begin immediately on the uphill task of regaining our credibility.

Neither he, nor any of the paper's executives, resigned. They promised to do better. Janet Cooke carried the can for all their failures.

Cooke sent back her Pulitzer a couple of weeks before the American Society of Newspaper Editors held its annual get-together. Bradlee argued that there was no defending yourself against, in his words, 'a pathological liar'. Others disagreed. Especially over the *Post*'s refusal to identify a young boy in danger.

■ Glass and Blair ■

It wasn't just young, ambitious reporters. At the end of the 1990s, another venerable American newspaper, the *Boston Globe*, discovered that one of its columnists, Patricia Smith, had made up the odd quote from the odd made-up individual. There was a system for checking on columnists' stuff, but mostly it was taken on trust. Trust.

In journalism, if a story is too good to be true, then more often than not it's too good to be true. A reporter from *Forbes.com* found that out the hard way trying to follow up a piece by a *wunderkind* magazine writer for *New Republic*, Stephen Glass.

The story was about a Californian software company called Jukt Micronics hiring a teenage hacker, 'Big Bad Bionic Boy', actually Ian Restil. It featured Ian's mum, Jamie, and Ian's representative – 'super-agent to super-nerds', Joe Hiert. Lobby group the National Assembly of Hackers and

TRUST ME, I'M A JOURNALIST

their president Frank Juliet were included too, as was Jim Ghort, the director of the Center for Interstate Online Investigations, and Julie Farthwork of the Computer Security Center. There were numbers or emails for all of them.

Forbes reporter Adam Penenberg wrote up how he went about checking up on Jukt after search engines threw up nothing:

> Our next step was to contact the Software Publishers Association of America. Nothing. Next on our list was the California Franchise Tax Board. An official from the Tax Board confirmed that Jukt Micronics had never paid any taxes. Further investigations revealed that Jukt Micronics, if it existed at all, was not listed under any of California's fifteen area codes. Sarah Gilmer from the office of the California Secretary of State said there was no record of the company, 'as a corporation, a limited liability or limited partnership'.

Jukt's phone number was a mobile belonging to Glass's brother. Jukt, like Ian and everyone else in the story, was a creation of Stephen Glass.

And Glass was creative. He had 'created' the First Church of George Herbert Walker Christ (Bush worshippers), the National Memorabilia Convention (selling Monica Lewinsky trinkets) and much, much more besides. The colourful nature of his crimes in a small circulation, elite magazine attracted the attention of Hollywood, which made a movie of it, called, a little predictably, *Shattered Glass*.

Glass wasn't the end of the run of scandal. In 2003, a few months before that film came out, this rather innocuous piece appeared in a Texan newspaper, the *San Antonio News-Express*:

> Words can't describe the emotions Juanita Anguiano has experienced since learning her 24-year-old son was missing 'somewhere in Iraq'.

So the single mother, a teacher's aide, points to the ceiling fan he installed in her small living room. She points to the pinstriped couches, the tennis bracelet still in its red velvet case and the Martha Stewart patio furniture, all gifts from her first born and only son. Her handyman, the man of her house.

Reporter Macarena Hernandez had gone to Los Fresnos to interview the mother of a soldier missing in Iraq. Juanita Anguiano's story attracted national attention. The *Boston Globe* sent a reporter to visit the 'white stucco duplex on the outskirts of a small town bounded by sugar cane and cotton fields'. So too did the *New York Times*. Its reporter wrote:

> Juanita Anguiano points proudly to the pinstriped couches, the tennis bracelet in its red case and the Martha Stewart furniture out on the patio. She proudly points up to the ceiling fan, the lamp for Mother's Day, the entertainment centre that arrived last Christmas and all the other gifts from her only son, Edward, a 24-year-old Army mechanic.

Sound familiar? It was almost as if the reporter had been following Macarena Hernandez around. Except that he'd never set foot in Los Fresnos. This was the work of a reporter whose personal and professional qualities were summed up like this by a colleague: 'He works like he lives, sloppily.'

Nothing as grandly imaginative as a heroin-addicted child caught out Jayson Blair. It was a complaint from another newspaper. Blair was in his late twenties. After being caught out lifting the Anguiano story, he quit. However, when the *New York Times* came to review his work they discovered that sloppy wasn't quite the word.

One of the most spectacular examples of Blair's *modus operandi* was a story he filed from West Virginia. It featured an interview conducted with the family of Jessica Lynch, while she was still missing in action:

> Mr Lynch seemed distracted as he stood on the porch of his hilltop home here looking into the tobacco fields and pastures.

The Lynch family home lies in a wooded valley. There are no tobacco fields or pastures on view. No wonder Mr Lynch was distracted. The report also featured many more examples of inventive reporting, including a dream from Jessica's mother and a basic misspelling of her name. Amazingly, though the views were mentioned not once but twice and they had read it, the family didn't complain about the story.

Blair's mobile phone records showed that he'd been in New York at the time the story was reported. A long way from the porch of the hilltop home.

So, were Cooke, Blair, Glass and all the other anti-heroes of journalism responsible for deepening the coastal shelf of media distrust? It would be nice to be able to pin the blame on journalists themselves. Then perhaps we could call for a moral revolution, a bit of reporterly backbone and trust could be restored and put back on the mantelpiece.

But, unfortunately according to a survey after the event, less than a third of the American public had ever heard of the Jayson Blair saga. The journalism scandals that rocked journalists failed to interest the public. *Shattered Glass* was a critical success, but made no money at the box office.

At the end of *Shattered Glass*, Glass's editor tells one of his friends and supporters on the magazine staff:

> We're all going to have to answer for what we let happen here. We're all going to have an apology to make … Every competitor we ever took a shot at, they're going to pounce, and they should. Because we blew it … He handed us fiction after fiction, and we printed them all as fact. Just because we found him entertaining.

So the question is less 'Can You Trust the Media?' Because the answer is quite obviously, 'no'. The question is whether it matters. Perhaps it does.

CHAPTER TWO

Trust and the BBC

There is one media institution in the UK that absolutely relies on the concept of trust, not least in its legal incarnation. The idea of a 'trust' as a legal instrument began in the Middle Ages. They were a means of keeping great estates together for future generations, to prevent dissolute heirs from squandering a family's fortune. The principle has been extended today to vouchsafe the quality and reliability of the pillar of the British media establishment, the BBC.

When the Beeb was put under pressure to reform itself to make it more responsive to outside criticism, trust probably seemed like a good word. So they used it.

The BBC exists thanks to a Royal Charter, renewed every ten years. The first charter was granted in the 1920s, when the BBC's first General Manager, John Reith, convinced the Prime Minister that a government takeover of the BBC, then a private company with a monopoly on radio broadcasts, would be against the national interest.

Royal charters were originally the mechanism by which monopolies were granted. The BBC, funded by its own tax, was unusual in that respect. That special levy gave it a kind of financial and editorial freedom, but also a strange position within the world of official bodies.

Taxation to support the BBC does not mean representation. The BBC's charter is not with British lawmakers in Parliament but with the executive: the Crown. This gives it a measure of political insulation too. Although politicians of all parties have viewed it with a mix of suspicion and resentment while in office, governments come and go within the ten-year cycle that determines its future.

Even amid a flood of privatisations in the 1980s, when Margaret Thatcher's government swept away public owner-ship of railways, airlines, energy and heavy industry, the BBC remained a licence-fee-funded island, dominating radio and claiming the lion's share of television audiences.

This happy situation might have continued but for Tony Blair's chief spinmeister, Alastair Campbell. Campbell, the head of communications at 10 Downing Street, was con-vinced, like his predecessors, that the corporation had a bias against the Labour Party.

Although Britain's newspaper press as a whole was res-olutely partisan, and mostly conservative, the BBC's charter obliged it to be fair and impartial in its news reporting. When a BBC reporter called Andrew Gilligan misrepre-sented a source to support a story many people felt was true – that the government had lied about the public case for invading Iraq – Campbell seized on his opportunity to con-front the BBC.

This particular battle over the public trust, with the gov-ernment on one side alleging bias and falsehood and the BBC on the other professing truth and journalistic integrity, illustrates just how complex the relationship between gov-ernment and the media is. How the media agenda acceler-ates and dominates itself. And how the cogs and wheels of modern public life can multiply small events into major catastrophes.

This particular catastrophe began with a short interview on Radio 4's *Today* programme one Thursday morning in 2003.

Today is perhaps the single most august media outlet in Britain. None of the UK's major newspapers or television programmes have anything like the seriousness and self-satisfaction of *Today*. It is the audio op-ed page for the capital's elite, a radio Star Chamber where leading politicians and visiting dignitaries are called to account over tea and toast. And its three hours of rolling news, interviews and debate are backed by the authority of the BBC with its 200 or so pages of editorial guidelines and its legal obligations to impartiality and accuracy.

In the official language of the corporation, its radio hosts 'are the public face and voice of the BBC's journalism. The tone and approach they take has a significant impact on perceptions of the BBC's accuracy and impartiality.' But the reality is very different. There's none of the deference, reserve and forelock-tugging you might expect from a broadcast that carries the BBC's imprimatur.

Today is a bear pit for presenters and interviewees. As *Today* presenter and BBC veteran John Humphrys told an audience: 'If we were not prepared to take on a very, very powerful government ... there would be no point in the BBC existing – that is ultimately what the BBC is for.'

Humphrys, too, was part of what made *Today* different. Confronted by critics of the 'liberal' media, his answer was blunt: 'Do we want to return to capital punishment or to see homosexuals persecuted? No. That is a broadly liberal position. And that's what the nation is. I bloody well hope the BBC is broadly liberal.'

Unsurprisingly, he has attracted damning criticism from both sides in British politics. Not all of them stood the test of time. A Conservative minister who accused Humphrys of 'poisoning the well of democratic debate' was later imprisoned for corruption.

A year after Tony Blair came to office, Alastair Campbell wrote to BBC bosses after one heated *Today* confrontation to complain that:

... the John Humphrys problem has assumed new proportions

after this morning's interview ... In response we have had a council of war and are now seriously considering whether, as a party, we will suspend co-operation when you make bids through us for government ministers.

But the scandal that mired *Today*, and threatened Humphrys once again, began not with the host himself, but with balding bachelor Andrew Gilligan. It was just after six in the morning on Thursday, 29 May 2003 when Gilligan, the programme's diplomatic correspondent, sounding only half-awake, did a radio two-way.

It was the morning Tony Blair hoped would be marked in the media as his triumphal entry into Basra – the first Western leader to visit defeated Iraq – and Humphrys was the studio anchor.

That Q&A began a process that ended with the suicide of one of the world's leading authorities on biological weapons and the removal of the BBC's two most powerful figures – Chairman Gavyn Davies and Director-General Greg Dyke.

It was a broadcast that led to an inquiry by one of Britain's most senior judges, Lord Hutton, and left a giant unresolved question mark hanging over the journalism of the world's biggest broadcast newsgatherer.

Gilligan's 6.07 a.m. report was based on a conversation of an hour or so a week before with Dr David Kelly over a coke and an apple juice (Gilligan had hung on to the receipt for £4.15, which he'd claimed on expenses – the price of his investigation). Kelly often met and talked to journalists. He'd been a weapons inspector in Iraq since the 1990s and a regular briefer of reporters. Gilligan himself was just back from a spell in Baghdad, reporting on the downfall of Saddam Hussein.

The exchange they had was probably quite similar to those Kelly had with other journalists, including some from the BBC. It touched on the September dossier, part of the case that the Blair administration had made against Saddam Hussein's regime. In the dossier, the British government had given the impression that some Iraqi chemical and biological weapons could be launched by missile within 45 minutes.

Kelly had proofread some of the dossier and had reservations about its contents, specifically the single sourcing of that 45-minute claim. Kelly, said Gilligan, told him this claim had been put into the dossier late, at the request of Downing Street's communications chief, Alastair Campbell, who had ordered that it be 'sexed up'.

A week after that meeting, Gilligan pitched the story to his editors at *Today*, recognising that Tony Blair's visit to Basra would provide an excellent news peg. Gilligan called late, after the normal editorial meeting had finished. He produced a brief radio script for a story to run at 7.30 a.m. that was approved but overnight, and following the usual format of the programme, he was also asked to do a brief, live, run-through just after 6 a.m.

Apparently, without an agreed script to hand, this became Gilligan's story on *Today*: that the British government had deliberately inserted information it knew to be false into the dossier, to make it more exciting and mislead the public. His source? 'One of the senior officials in charge of drawing up that document.'

The scale of the BBC is so vast that Gilligan estimated he made nineteen different appearances on its news outlets that day. The story was carried on everything from music radio stations to the nightly news. Downing Street was furious.

A day or so later Gilligan wrote an account for a conservative tabloid that was headlined: 'I asked my intelligence source why Blair misled us all over Saddam's weapons. His reply? One word … CAMPBELL.'

Kelly had expressed himself rather more cautiously to another BBC journalist, Susan Watts, in a taped phone call that covered much the same ground as Gilligan's meeting. In that conversation, Kelly didn't describe the dossier as having been 'sexed up'. Instead he said that the 'word-smithing is actually quite important ... Sometimes you've got to put things into words that the public will understand.'

Gilligan quoted those words in an email to two MPs, when he revealed that David Kelly was Susan Watts' source.

The difference in those two accounts, the fact that Gilligan 'lost' a manuscript version of the notes of his meeting, and the changes he made to records kept on a personal organiser, led Lord Hutton to observe: 'I have considerable doubt as to how reliable Mr Gilligan's evidence is as regards what Dr Kelly said to him.'

So how did *Today*, with its millions of listeners and the power of the BBC behind it, become beholden to Andrew Gilligan and his questionable note-taking skills?

The programme had gone on the air in the late 1950s, bringing listeners what were genteelly described as 'topical talks'. It had never been particularly interested in reporting. But over the years its focus had shifted; it no longer discussed the morning's newspaper stories. Instead, it engaged in agenda-setting, pre-empting the day's big political stories by inviting government ministers to reveal all ahead of their appointments in Parliament. In return for publicity, they had to submit themselves to the kinds of cross-examination that even the raucous proceedings of the House of Commons found hard to match.

In the late 1990s, the agenda-setting process accelerated with the arrival of editor Rod Liddle. Labelled a 'priapic boy racer' by one rather unimpressed political journalist, *Today*'s new boss was an unkempt controversialist with a passing resemblance to The Cure's Robert Smith. Liddle wanted *Today* to do more than just jump the gun on politics. He wanted to force the government to react to stories that *Today* was breaking.

Although the British Broadcasting Corporation employs thousands of journalists, most of them are not routinely in the business of making the news. It does have distinguished and renowned investigative reporters on its payroll, but mostly they produce documentaries rather than servicing the needs of a hungry daily news outfit, on air for three hours each weekday morning.

To change *Today*, Liddle needed a new type of reporter, unbound by the staid conventions of BBC journalism. A year into his editorship he hired Andrew Gilligan from right-of-centre broadsheet the *Sunday Telegraph*.

Gilligan already had a reputation as a reporter who delivered, although that came with a caveat. As one of his bosses later remarked: 'You slightly raised your eyebrows at times, wondering if things were really true.' Bringing someone in from outside the BBC was a risk, but Liddle liked to take risks. And *Today*'s defence and diplomatic correspondent was soon bringing in stories that riled Downing Street, delivering exactly what Liddle wanted – a reputation for muckraking.

Ironically, it was Liddle, not Gilligan, who ran into trouble first. *Today*'s editor had a problem keeping his opinions to himself. While editor, he began writing a column for the *Guardian* and when one commentary effectively urged readers to vote Labour, he fell foul of the BBC's editorial guidelines on impartiality. Senior managers insisted Liddle choose between a future inside the corporation, or outside as a commentator and, with a contract on offer, he chose the latter.

His replacement on the programme was Kevin Marsh who took up his post at the end of 2002. Marsh was a serious and experienced editor who had joined the BBC in 1978 – the temperamental opposite of his flamboyant predecessor. In 1997, when Alastair Campbell assumed – mistakenly – that Marsh would apply for the editorship of *Today*, he had personally attacked *The World at One* editor in an extraordinary five-page diatribe to the head of BBC News. Marsh was accused of consistent bias against the government, of being 'closed to reason' and of following an 'anti-Labour follow-any-old-Tory-guff-agenda'.

Marsh was wary of Gilligan, but Gilligan had a powerful ally in John Humphrys and taking over the BBC's flagship broadcast in the build-up to a war brought *Today*'s editor bigger problems than keeping an eye on a lone reporter.

Most of Marsh's problems still came from *Today*'s interviews. Tony Blair's spokesman and de facto chief of staff, Alastair Campbell, was a regular correspondent, filing a dozen written complaints about *Today* in the run-up to the Iraq war. The complaint over Gilligan, unluckily, was number thirteen. So when it came, Marsh and his bosses were used to being under attack. Their response to yet more government criticism was to back Gilligan and go into instant defence.

That line ran right to the very summit of the BBC. Both Chairman Gavyn Davies and Director-General Greg Dyke had been keen Labour supporters. Davies' wife worked on the personal staff of then Chancellor Gordon Brown. Dyke had been a party donor. Both men took the challenge from Campbell as a chance to demonstrate their political independence.

His bosses may have put up the barricades, but Andrew Gilligan wasn't the kind of reporter to be backward in coming forward. When David Kelly was called to appear before a Select Committee, Gilligan emailed suggested lines of enquiry to two of the members. Under questioning, Kelly lied about his contact with another BBC journalist. It was a lie that would have been quickly and easily exposed, damaging his credibility and threatening his job and pension. Shortly after the hearing he killed himself.

But the legacy of Gilligan's casual reporting, far from undermining him or the BBC, or questioning the evidential principles of good reporting, has been quite remarkable. Andrew Gilligan resigned from the BBC saying, 'Most of my story was right.' He is now a successful television presenter, newspaper columnist and reporter on London's *Evening Standard*.

The BBC's own journalists produced a coruscating documentary on the Gilligan story – accusing their own management of 'betting the farm' on a shaky foundation. With Maoist self-criticism, the *Panorama* programme broadcast a withering attack on their own colleagues and management before Lord Hutton had even produced his report.

So what saved the BBC? Although Andrew Gilligan resigned, John Humphrys stayed at the heart of *Today*. He remained publicly convinced that Gilligan's story was right. As he told one journalist in the aftermath of Hutton: 'It's wrong to suggest we'll change because a judge said we made a mistake.' His interviews are as combative as ever.

Hutton exonerated the government but found Gilligan unreliable. The pillars of managerial support that the BBC had constructed on this rather shaky foundation collapsed. Davies resigned and Dyke was effectively forced out by the board that Davies had chaired.

But the Hutton Inquiry was not popular. To begin with, its chairman Brian Hutton was a dry Ulsterman, whom critics saw as an establishment figure.

There had been a strong vein of public opposition to the invasion of Iraq. More than a million people had demonstrated against it in London. The question marks over Gilligan's reporting were seen as matters of detail. The wider feeling was that he and the BBC had challenged the government over Iraq and were now being punished for it. Ousted Director-General Greg Dyke made no secret of his belief that this was in fact the case.

A poll following Hutton's findings found 55 per cent of respondents agreeing that it had been a 'whitewash'. Hutton demonstrated that Gilligan's reporting was unreliable, but the public deemed that the doubts he had aired over WMD were right. Despite the government being cleared of any wrongdoing, trust in Tony Blair's leadership following the inquiry slumped by nearly a quarter.

The process of rebuilding the BBC was all about re-establishing trust, so that is exactly what the government did – it established a Trust.

▌ In Trusts we trust ▌

Under Greg Dyke and Gavyn Davies, the BBC had been run by a charismatic showman and overseen by a slightly reserved intellectual. Post-Hutton those roles were reversed. Mark Thompson, a journalist who had risen up through the BBC's executive ranks and done a spell running Channel 4, returned as Director-General. Michael Grade, the cigar-chewing scion of a British showbiz family, came in as Chairman of Governors.

The two men faced the task of renegotiating the Royal Charter with a government their predecessors had confronted.

One of the answers was a new governance structure. The government wanted a body that would be more responsive to outside complaints, less uncritically supportive of BBC management. They got it. The old BBC Board of Governors that Grade had chaired was to be replaced by a BBC Trust. Governors would become trustees. Grade would continue as Chairman.

The name change satisfied the government, but industry figures were more sceptical – one compared it to the re-branding of Britain's ageing nuclear power station from Windscale to Sellafield. Not much else but the name was changed.

The BBC's obsession with 'trust', its use in speeches, documents and even as a name, had begun earlier with the work of economist and former BBC Chairman, Gavyn Davies.

At the beginning of the 1990s, Davies had been commissioned by the BBC to come up with a formal justification for the renewal of the BBC's charter. He teamed up with his old tutorial supervisor from Oxford, Andrew Graham. Graham had helped Davies before. As an economist for the Wilson government in the 1970s he had helped bring Davies to Downing Street as an adviser. But by the time Labour lost power in 1979, Graham was back in Balliol and Davies was contemplating a transfer of his economic skills to the world of investment banking.

Despite being economists, the two men argued that the BBC was necessary for political reasons, namely democracy and empowerment. They said that 'central to the idea of the democratic society is that of the well-informed and self-determining individual', and what was more, 'a fully functioning democracy requires a public service broadcaster.'

What did that mean? 'There has to be a source of information which can be trusted to be accurate in its news, documentaries and current affairs programmes and to be impartial between social and political views.'

The public didn't just need accurate and impartial information, the two argued; they needed a 'trusted' provider. Later on, Andrew Graham spelled that message out even more clearly: 'What is needed from a public interest point of view is a source of information that is impartial and trusted.'

Accuracy and impartiality were highly contested issues. Neither was easily measured or monitored. The BBC had never been happy measuring its success in ratings, terms that commercial advertisers understood. But 'trust' could be gauged by polling. Here was a direct measure of the value of public service broadcasting.

It took time for trust to filter into the corporate language of the BBC. By the 2000s, the change was detectable in the promotion of BBC News. In the 1990s, the news had been billed in annual reports as 'authoritative'. Now, that label was dumped for one that was shorter, neater and came with numbers – 'trust'.

With trust, the BBC could be measured by the same yardstick that pollsters applied to politicians. Dominating online, radio and television, the BBC's content commanded by far the biggest share of voice in Britain's crowded media. The poll ratings followed.

As BBC Chairman, Michael Grade could proudly announce that 80 per cent of the British public trusted BBC News – more than they trusted any other rival.

But just two years later, Grade had switched jobs to one of those rivals, the BBC's main commercial competitor ITV, and the wheels had come off the trust wagon. This time it wasn't the news, it was a combination of events that began with children's pets. When children's programme *Blue Peter* had first conceived of adopting a pet, back in 1962, a puppy was bought for viewers to name. It died after one TV appearance so the producers managed to find a similar dog in a pet shop. Viewers named the dog Petra.

But more than 40 years later, when a competition to name a pet cat produced the winning answer Cookie (thought to be the result of an internet prank campaign), the name was switched to the runner-up, Socks. When the news got out, an orgy of condemnation and self-flagellation ensued. Except this time from kids.

CHAPTER THREE

Media Bulimia: How the media has come to dominate us

What, exactly, is the media? There is a simple answer and one that most reasonable people would volunteer, if pressed. The media is how we become informed. It's how the citizens of a democracy keep tabs on their government. It's how consumers find out the truth about big corporations. The media's job is to dose us up with all the facts we need to function. The media is a public trust.

Wrong answer. *Nul points.*

The media is not in the information supply business. It is in the distraction business. It wants to occupy the seconds, minutes and hours of our lives that are not spent earning the money required to make us valuable to businesses as a consumer or governments as a taxpayer, and as much of our working time as it can. It is there to force itself into our consciousness and by doing so, live another day.

And to claim that headspace, the media is prepared to do almost anything. It will purvey naked flesh, stock prices, sexual impropriety or political analysis, all in the hope of securing our precious attention. An important way of getting into our heads is by selecting those things that are new or unusual or presenting the familiar in novel ways. In shorthand, the news.

The 'news' is presented in all manner of ways. Publications like *The Week* sell themselves – paradoxically – on the amount of time they will save you, through filtering a week's worth of news. Twenty-four-hour news channels exist permanently in the present, relating incremental developments to running stories live, or else circulating small bursts of news in a format called 'the wheel'.

British newspapers sell themselves on opinionated reportage, American papers on neurotic objectivity. Talk radio, beloved of cab drivers the world over, allows us to drive while we listen and even argue back. Anything, anything, anything at all, but let's have your attention.

If you thought this was a simple case of theft, you'd be wrong again. Our time is not stolen by the media. This is an inside job and we are willing participants in the robbery.

The media is first and foremost an enterprise that is interested in putting metrics on the value of us, our time and the nature of our relationship with whatever they have conjured up to occupy it.

Commercial media execs study circulation figures, unique users, ratings. They want to sell on their relationship with us in exchange for advertising money or sponsorship. Government-funded services like the BBC try to quantify that relationship to justify their share of the public purse to politicians, interest groups and the public themselves.

How much we're worth depends on who we are. We are segmented by age, income, job, interests, sex, life stage, household – the list is as detailed as the customer requires. Advertisers want access to people who will purchase their products. Politicians want to keep swing voters happy.

Different media measure our time differently. Our television deals in audience share, as well as viewing figures or ratings. Online execs argue over the value of page impressions and unique users. Radio measures itself by listeners and by 'reach' – the number of people who can actually access it. So too do the news channels, with their modest audiences. Newspapers live or die by circulation; time is at the disposal of the buyer, the cover price gains us admission.

Then there's the quality of that elusive 'relationship'. How do we feel about the media? Do we regard it with hostility and suspicion, or warmth and fuzziness? It's by measuring these feelings that we are brought to things like trust, and those things are measured by opinion polling.

Trust is an extra characteristic with which to differentiate a channel from its rivals. At the beginning of the 1960s, the American TV industry used polling on trust to claim that broadcasters were more trusted than news-papers. At the turn of the 21st century, the BBC used trust to help its campaign for continued government funding.

So the media, whether it relies on government handouts, wooing advertisers or subscriptions, is in the business of getting your time and trading it, or in the language of business, 'monetising' it. It's that simple and that complicated.

Back in 1925, before it was gobbled up by Rupert Murdoch, the *Wall Street Journal* published an op-ed entitled 'A Fictitious Public Interest'. According to the *Journal*'s leader writers then:

> A newspaper is a private enterprise, owing nothing whatever to the public, which grants it no franchise. It is therefore 'affected' with no public interest. It is emphatically the property of its owner, who is selling a manufactured product at his own risk.

The same is, more or less, true of newspapers today. But things are a bit more complicated in television land.

▋ The Niagara of news ▋

We are currently wealthy, fat, comfortable and complacent. We have currently a built-in allergy to unpleasant or disturbing information. Our mass media reflect this. But unless we get up off our fat surpluses and recognise that television in the main is being used to distract, delude, amuse and insulate us, then television and those who finance it, those who look at it and those who work at it, may see a totally different picture too late.

When legendary American journalist Edward R. Murrow gave that cheery message to the Radio and Television News Directors' Association in Chicago in 1958, his employer, CBS, ran just fifteen minutes of news in primetime, before shows like *Name That Tune* and *Leave It To Beaver*.

Until a couple of years before, NBC's news programme had been *Camel News Caravan*, sponsored by a tobacco company. Among the cigarette-maker's demands was a ban on shots of 'No Smoking' signs. The newscaster – who doubled up as host of *What's My Line* – was obliged to present the day's stories while holding a lit cigarette. And Camel insisted too that no one featured in the news should be shown smoking a cigar – Winston Churchill being the sole exception.

Murrow was a smoker, but he was also an idealist. In an age of just three television networks, he imagined that the public might be educated and informed through the triumphant medium of television, if only by seizing command of the airwaves and providing more news and current affairs.

Half a century later, a British journalist – as iconic in his way as Murrow – took to an industry stage to deliver a damning verdict on a world where news was now ubiquitous:

If you're not careful, eventually, you get to a point where you just think 'what is the point of watching this stuff?' I have been a television journalist for almost all my working life. And I have to confess to a gnawing anxiety. Does exposing people to this ceaseless torrent make them any better off? I have always believed passionately – and continue to believe – in the public's right to know, that a well-informed democracy is a healthy democracy – but you do begin to wonder when this ceaseless tide of pre-digested stuff comes at you.

That was Jeremy Paxman, presenter of one of Britain's best-known current affairs programmes, *Newsnight*. He got the job in 1989, the year Sky News launched as Britain's first 24-hour news channel. Sky News added another 8,500 hours to the volume of news produced in Britain each year. This is just part of the explosion in news that has happened over that time. As Paxman himself pointed out in 1995, the year before Tony Blair took office, the BBC alone broadcast just over 5,000 hours of news. Just ten years later that figure had more than doubled to 12,500 hours.

Today, British television viewers can still watch Sky, but they can also get 24-hour news in English from the BBC, EuroNews, France 24, Deutsche-Welle TV, Al Jazeera English, Russia Today, Fox News, CNN, NDTV and many more. Paxman too has changed direction. He is now a high-brow quiz show host as well as a journalist – for *What's My Line*, read *University Challenge*.

Back in the 1950s, Murrow wanted to interrupt the entertainment streaming into people's homes to 'reflect occasionally the hard, unyielding realities of the world in which we live'. He was concerned that viewers might amuse themselves to death, insulated from global political problems that carried the threat of nuclear annihilation.

Today Paxman contemplates a veritable Niagara of news, worried not that people have no access to the information that they need to be informed, but that the sheer volume of television news has corrupted both the spectacle and the spectators. Constant exposure to the flood leaves people confused and apathetic, watching pictures with the volume turned down.

There's no doubt that there is a vast amount of news being churned out by broadcasters of all hues. But does the public watch these channels? The most successful of them, the BBC's offering, gets less than 1 per cent of the total television audience. Even though you can now catch news channels on the train to the airport or glance at their headlines on giant public screens or online, their ubiquity is not matched by their viewing figures. As the number of news providers has proliferated, audiences have fragmented, leaving none with the critical mass they would need to claim power, authority or even trustworthiness.

Nearly ten years ago Hal Varian, a professor of information at Berkeley, wrote a paper called *Markets for Information Goods*. It's none too elegantly expressed but it explains why, as more news is produced, less and less of it becomes significant:

> I would like to coin a 'Malthus's law' of information. Recall that Malthus noted that the number of stomachs grew geometrically but the amount of food grew linearly ... the supply of information (in virtually every medium) grows exponentially whereas the amount that is consumed grows at best linearly. This is ultimately due to the fact that our mental powers and time available to process information is constrained. This has the uncomfortable consequence that the fraction of the information produced that is actually consumed is asymptoting towards zero.

In other words, news was more important for people when there was fifteen minutes of it before *Leave It To Beaver* than it is now, when it's in your face on the train, in the pub and in business meetings.

▊ Political playthings ▊

Two things have driven the explosion in television news channels: cheaper technology and political ambition. CNN's global dominance as a conduit for news in the first Gulf

War had politicians around the world green with envy. Satellites and bandwidth have made distribution and sharing material easier than ever. France 24 was a dream of Jacques Chirac; the French parliament said it was necessary to counter Anglo-Saxon 'cultural imperialism'. Qatar's rulers bankroll Al Jazeera. Iran funds PRESS TV and Russia Today is a division of that country's state-run news agency.

Popular demand for news has not driven this oversupply. Like wine lakes and butter mountains, the television news glut is the result of political intervention.

But just as growing supplies of year-round fruit and vegetables air-freighted onto supermarket shelves have failed to realise nutritionists' dreams of a well-nourished nation, so endless supplies of news have failed to bring about what every high-minded journalist says they want, a well-informed and politically-engaged public.

The reason is pretty simple if you think of acquiring political news as an economic choice, which is to say one about rationing a scarce resource – your time. Political news is low on intrinsic enjoyment (except for hobbyists, e.g. members of political parties). There isn't much fun to be had weighing up policy and spending choices in education, healthcare and prisons. It isn't very socially useful either, except for elites (the 'chattering classes'), because you can't share it widely. Nor is it economically useful, because the value of decision-making based on political information – your vote – is individually almost worthless. This leads to what political theorists call rational ignorance.

Faced with the low relative value of political news, people choose information primarily for its entertainment, or personal usefulness (known in the trade as 'news you can use'). This can take in everything from sports coverage to gardening tips, health to personal finance. And, of course, salacious stories of wasted celebrities and real-life crime.

The Niagara of news has consequences not just for people's viewing habits and their respect for the media, but also for the media providers themselves – mostly commercial ones. In short, more news means fewer profits.

Television news has a long tradition of losing money. In 1965, in the middle of what is sometimes called television's golden age, the chairman of CBS, Bill Paley, told his shareholders, with regret, that profits had dropped slightly owing to coverage of unscheduled news events, like rocket launches, civil rights marches and the funeral of Winston Churchill. Earnings were down by six cents a share.

News may have been important to the public but it was a drag on the bottom line. As David Halberstam noted in his critique of Paley's corporation, *The Power and the Profits*:

> Though more than 60 per cent of the American people say that television is their prime carrier of the news and information, CBS Inc. does not by a long shot think that CBS News is 60 per cent of its self. Aside from the half-hour evening news show, CBS News had access to only 4 per cent of the prime time schedule ... in contrast to 26 per cent for situation comedies, 12 per cent for adventure and mysteries, and 16 per cent for feature films.

For networks and the corporations that owned them, news was the price of advertising riches. Delivered with enough solemnity it bought off unwelcome attention from regulators. As a network boss from the 1970s admitted:

> Making money from news was thought to be a very bad idea. The thinking was that if you are a broadcaster and charged with performing a public service, it was a good idea to be able to tell the [regulator], 'Well I do make all this money, but on the other hand, I have to be able to support our big loss leader, the news division'. And if your big loss leader, to which you are making large, financial contributions to serve the public, is

making money, it doesn't look like you're doing all that much of a public service, does it?

But impartiality was not just a regulatory requirement. It was the requirement of a mass audience. The clue is not in 'cast', it's in 'broad'. When TV news channels attracted vast swathes of the viewing public, alienating viewers with tub-thumping partisan television news was not a clever move. Consensus was fired into every line of electrons on the television screen. And when that consensus shifted, as it did over the war in Vietnam, the consequences were devastating.

◾ Cheaper news, more news ◾

Back in the day, television news was power. At the beginning of the 1990s, when a presidential address to announce the invasion of Panama interrupted a daytime soap opera – *The Bold and the Beautiful* – a colleague of mine on CBS's foreign desk took a call from an outraged viewer.

'Ma'am,' she responded, brimful of scorn, 'if you don't think hearing from the President of the United States is more important than some crappy soap opera, you don't deserve to watch television.'

Those were the days. To work in television was to sit in judgement, a judgement prescribed by codes and tradition, but that wasn't the point. Television journalism stood with its hand on the great sluice gate of stories and information, turning a flood into a trickle that could be poured into the homes of millions.

We didn't know it then, but talking back to viewers was the high-water mark of power as far as broadcast news was concerned. In fact the economics of news on television had been changing since the moment Ted Turner launched his Cable News Network (CNN) in 1980. CBS staffers had referred to it as Chicken Noodle News and although Turner nearly went bust in the first couple of years, by the mid-1980s CNN was making money.

Never mind the satellite technical gubbins, on the broadcast side CNN's only innovation was to stretch every formula and cliché of television news across 24 hours. Despite its comparatively tiny audience, CNN still kept to the conventions and traditions of mass media American broadcast journalism.

By the time the 24-hour TV news concept was a proven commercial success, and with the economics of cable subscription clear, those conventions were looking like a straitjacket.

With niche audiences, being partisan was suddenly an attractive commercial proposition. Without having to pander to the masses in the middle, broadcasters could appeal to people who resented that cosy consensus. One man, a right-wing Republican strategist called Roger Ailes, knew exactly who they were. And he knew exactly the man to put money into reaching them.

When Rupert Murdoch started Fox News in the 1990s, he paid several stations ten dollars a subscriber just to carry the channel. Paying for a place on the set-top box was unheard of. Ten years on, Fox had become the top-ranked news channel, able to command a dozen dollars a year from each and every subscriber.

Cable and satellite opened up more channels but they also fragmented audiences. When America's most trusted man, Walter Cronkite, stepped down from newscasting, 17 million people watched the CBS Evening News. Twenty-five years later, barely 6 million were tuning in to his next-successor-but-one, Katie Couric.

When businessman Mel Karmazin took over an ailing CBS he toyed with the idea of buying CNN and dispensing with his costly news division altogether. When asked later for his thoughts on how to fix the still flagging CBS Evening News, he answered:

What would I do with the CBS Evening News? I challenged everybody when I was there. I said, 'Let's eliminate it'. You know, I mean who cares? The issue was that that became impractical because if you're a network, you've got to have a news organization.

The pressure on national and international news budgets was all downwards. Cable, satellite and then broadband didn't just fragment audiences. They took away the regulatory argument that had insisted broadcasting was special because limited airwaves meant a limited number of channels.

Unit costs meant bosses wanted more for their money. Why have journalists waiting around to service a half-hour nightly news programme when the same team, studios and equipment could supply stories around the clock?

In the 1990s, NBC started an all-news network to amortise the costs of its network news division. In Britain, ITN tried the same with the short-lived ITN News Channel. But in the UK, with the BBC offering 24-hour news free-to-air, a subscription news channel wasn't going to make money. In fact Britain's biggest commercial network, ITV, spent the 1990s returning profits to shareholders by forcing down the price of its news contract. It dropped from nearly £70 million a year in the mid-1990s to just £30 million a year by the 2000s.

As news became more widely available on specialist channels, the arguments for interrupting programming in favour of unscheduled news events decreased. The first beneficiary of this lack of interest in the news was CNN. In 1986, it was alone in covering the launch of the shuttle Challenger. Network executives were bored with NASA. When the shuttle's tanks exploded, only CNN carried the story live.

Still, CNN existed then, as now, on tiny audiences in comparison to those available to the networks, because although barely anyone tuned in at a given time, it reached a great swathe of viewers.

▌ Live ▐

The growing technical sophistication of live broadcasting was also changing the game. One of the most compelling and awful commentaries of the radio age had been the Hindenburg tragedy in the 1930s, when an airship had exploded and the broadcast that was supposed to celebrate its successful arrival turned into an eyewitness report of a disaster.

Now television could go yet further and bring the images of deaths of astronauts live into the world's homes and offices. It wasn't just set-piece events either. The invention of flyaway satellite dishes meant that broadcasters could go to places never previously seen and show events unfolding live. They could swap pictures by satellite news exchanges instantaneously.

But the biggest change in live technology was that it made television cheap. A reporter on the end of a live link could talk and talk and talk. A camera could wander while a commentary was kept up. Twenty-four-hour news television became the art of speculative analysis, picking over live images that viewers had almost as much chance of interpreting as the studio presenters themselves; and when the pictures ran out it could resort to discussion, trading opinion in the rather muted tradition of broadcast news.

Cheap news made possible niche news. The enormous costs of broadcasting need no longer be spread across massive networks. Although CNN had shown that a standalone TV news network was possible, it took Roger Ailes and Rupert Murdoch to take the genre to the next level.

It was when the Fox News Channel brought the techniques of talk radio to the staid studios of television news that the formula was reinvented. Instead of phone-ins and the possibility of dull contributions from the audience, live newsgathering could be endlessly riffed on by presenters and pundits without ever reaching a conclusion. Talk news TV didn't want to dispense information, just to keep the audience that little bit longer with live shots interspersed by outspoken and entertaining opinion. Where Fox led, CNN and MSNBC followed. The temple of television news had been sacked.

In Britain, editors embraced the changes grudgingly. More news was live and reporters took on the role of pundits. The best of them were trusted to surf the wave of regulation on impartiality that governed British broadcasting. The worst brought down accusations of bias in reporting the Middle East, business and security at large.

More news outlets meant that news, once tightly rationed, was commoditised. The marketing and promotions departments of mainstream broadcasters didn't want to promote news programmes, preferring to spend their time luring people to primetime entertainment.

News editors were reduced to boosting their own products, coming up with gimmicks – new ways to present and deliver the news – anything that would provide a reason for other journalists who reported on the media to write about the changing face of broadcast news, what politicians called 'free media'. Some of these gimmicks were good, some bad.

Channel Five, my own under-resourced station, was famous for them. Our first attempt at making the headlines was to have Kirsty Young present the news standing up or perched on the front of a desk, papers in hand. We replaced labour-intensive news packages with studio chats and video clips. It wasn't just shameless attention-grabbing. Our budget was a fraction of the money then being put into rival news services. We simply couldn't afford to reproduce the carefully crafted miniature films and complex graphics packages of our competitors.

One of my own innovations was 'classic reporting', a marketing exercise that grouped veteran TV reporters together for the purposes of an advertising poster. The channel was rebranding itself as serious and the reports themselves were exactly that, not the kind of thing that would generate noise or controversy. One of my successors got more attention by banning 'noddies', the insertion of a nodding presenter cut into interviews when editing.

But attention didn't necessarily bring viewers. Other non-news television programmes were able to offer live rows over simulated sex or racist bullying. Programmes like *Big Brother*, *I'm A Celebrity ... Get Me Out Of Here!* and *The Apprentice* borrowed from the observational tradition of documentaries and carried their own discussion shows – like *The Apprentice: You're Fired!* and the imaginatively titled *I'm A Celebrity ... Get Me Out Of Here Now!* – extending onto other channels and airing the very issues and confrontations they had manufactured.

Unlike drama or entertainment, the news was unreliable. Big stories ran against one another and then disappeared. Brief, functional introductions to news stories meant there was little room for an on-screen personality with which to engage. With only modest budgets, compared to newspapers, there was virtually no chance of television being able to 'buy up' stories. The technologies and techniques that news had pioneered were now being deployed more successfully and on a grander scale by 'factual' programmes that did not carry the onerous burdens of the genre. Only problem was, as we saw in chapter one, corners were cut.

And what did it mean for people on the receiving end? Surprisingly little. As news became more available it did not lead to a wave of information-cravers addicted to every incremental development in every story. Television news had traded on scarcity value. When satellite and cable spread it across every second of the day, its ubiquity did not feed a mass obsession with public affairs, or even with the modest selection of stories that were squeezed into bulletins, or re-circulated on 24-hour running orders. It simply allowed people the convenience of opting out.

▌ The 1 per cent rule ▐

Viewers were changing too; they were turning their back on television. Veteran BBC correspondent John Simpson observed:

> We have popularised our reporting and our agenda: that hasn't worked. We have tried a dozen facelifts and re-launches: no good. We have dropped some of our best presenters and brought in young, attractive people, who have done nothing to increase the ratings.
>
> ... In an age when no one disapproves if you are ignorant about the world, and where reality seems less important to the programme-makers than reality shows, television news shouldn't try so hard to attract an audience that it will probably never see again.

If television journalists were giving up, then cheap consumer electronics and broadband connections had given their old audience the opportunity to jump right into the gap.

Now they could record, edit and share video on all kinds of devices. Sites like YouTube allowed them to air and share material. The only thing they lacked was the time and motivation to produce anything worth watching and, once created, the money to market it.

Online commentators coined the '1 per cent rule'. As one executive at Yahoo! noted, in the company's discussion forums:

> 1 per cent of the user population might start a group; 10 per cent of the user population might participate actively, and actually author content, whether starting a thread or respond-

ing to a thread-in-progress; 100 per cent of the user population benefits from the activities of the above groups.

Which is a nice way of saying people are more interested in viewing than doing.

The spread of technology had increased the likelihood of pictures being made available. But although technology had transformed the recording, storing and sharing of images, it had done nothing to change the ground glass lens through which those images were captured.

The technology gave most power to those with the ability to create stories, and that was neither journalists nor the public at large. Instead, its most effective proponents became terrorist groups, using it to video the murders of hostages, some gruesome, some simply cold-blooded. Or to stage murderous displays like 9/11. It was a cause for despair rather than optimism.

Technology did allow some professional journalists to escape what they thought of as corporate constraints. Broadband is holding out some hope for lovers of supposedly objective, non-partisan news not dependent on sponsors or a broader political agenda. Paul Jay, a Canadian broadcaster, quit his job as producer of a long-running political debate show on the Canadian Broadcasting Corporation to write a fictional film, *Kandahar* – a political conspiracy set in 2020. But when the full horror of the futuristic plot revealed itself, he says he realised how close the world is coming to disaster and that broadcasters and journalists were not helping the situation.

'After 9/11, you could see the complete capitulation of American television to a political agenda that was extremely dangerous,' he says. 'It started to occur to me it was like I was living in the 1920s and looking ahead to 1939. I thought, Gee, I don't want to be in 1939 and say to myself what could I have done about this in the twenties?'

So he started an online TV channel. Cheap digital technology means Jay can put vast volumes of news produced by a global network of high quality stringers onto the internet. The channel, *therealnews.com*, aims to be directly supported by the audience, not through a licence fee but through a few dollars a month subscription. That's a lot to pay just for news in a world already saturated by broadcasting. But the website is an impressive demonstration of intent, with a bold shaming of conventional television news 'failures' and a plan to 'change the economics of television journalism' by refusing sponsorship and advertising.

Whether it will work or not remains to be seen. But it shows that trust – in this case, the ability to trust the commercial and political independence of news providers – is seen by some as a holy grail. And as our attention has moved online, so the quest for trust has moved there too.

CHAPTER FOUR

Answering Back: The online explosion of media

It is hard to overstate the impact of digital technologies and the internet on the media.

Yes, it is a very tired cliché, so 1999, but it is as universally transforming as Gutenberg's invention of moveable type. There's a reason why they call it the digital revolution. I'm a believer. You can read my blog (adrianmonck.blogspot. com) about it every day.

Later in this book (chapter eight) I argue that Gutenberg's revolution paved the way for the media to take the place of religion in our lives. Today, the digital revolution has paved the way for the media to *dominate* our lives. From blogs with an average readership of six through to your Facebook pages with hundreds of friends, to bbc.co.uk with hundreds of millions of users, we are now connected to what is going on in the world – the news – in a way we never have been. My kids will live their lives online.

Commercially, there isn't a single established media company that has figured out the online world and if they say they have, they are lying.

That is their problem, though. Beyond that, the web and everything that is going on it poses fundamental questions for our notions of trust, particularly in relation to the media. In essence, though, those questions are not that dissimilar to the issues we have already looked at in the 'old' media, in particular in the news. And these questions are as old as the media itself. At least as old as the internet.

▮▮ You're a dog – user contributions and trust ▮▮

The *New Yorker* magazine is famous for the quirky nature of its cartoons. About twenty drawings make it into each edition, each intended to be enjoyed and forgotten. Some, though, are destined to endure a little longer, like one by Peter Steiner from 1993. Steiner's cartoon has a dog sitting by a computer screen. The dog turns to his canine companion sitting beside him and explains that, on the internet, 'Nobody knows you're a dog'.

On the internet, in other words, nobody knows when you're lying.

In the case of an august old media publication such as the *New Yorker*, it's not just the cartoons that are famous – it's the accuracy and elegance of the writing. *New Yorker* contributors are not just required to be prose stylists, they're also, famously, asked to justify every line of their work to fact-checkers.

Who better, then, than the *New Yorker* to explore the internet phenomenon of Wikipedia? Wikipedia was launched in 2001, an online encyclopaedia whose pages are written and edited by whoever wants to write and edit them. Wikipedia has its rules, but openness is fundamental to both its success and its abuse.

In 2006, the *New Yorker* published an article by Stacy Schiff called 'Know it all: Can Wikipedia conquer expertise?'. According to the piece:

One regular on the site is a user known as Essjay, who holds a PhD in theology and a degree in canon law and has written or contributed to sixteen thousand entries. A tenured professor of religion at a private university, Essjay made his first edit in February 2005. Initially, he contributed to articles in his field – on the penitential rite, transubstantiation, the papal tiara. Soon he was spending fourteen hours a day on the site, though he was careful to keep his online life a secret from his colleagues and friends. (To his knowledge, he has never met another Wikipedian, and he will not be attending Wikimania, the second international gathering of the encyclopaedia's contributors, which will take place in early August in Boston.)

Gradually, Essjay found himself devoting less time to editing and more to correcting errors and removing obscenities from the site. In May, he twice removed a sentence from the entry on Justin Timberlake asserting that the pop star had lost his home in 2002 for failing to pay federal taxes – a statement that Essjay knew to be false.

Schiff was no ingénue. In 1995, she'd been shortlisted for a prestigious Pulitzer Prize for her biography of Antoine de Saint-Exupéry, and in 2000 she won one for her life of Vera Nabokov. She had numerous prestigious academic fellowships and was hardly a jobbing reporter. The *New Yorker* too was famous for its tradition of checking everything. Essjay himself was pretty powerful when it came to checking things:

> Essjay is serving a second term as chair of the mediation committee. He is also an admin, a bureaucrat, and a checkuser, which means that he is one of fourteen Wikipedians authorized to trace I.P. addresses in cases of suspected abuse. He often takes his laptop to class, so that he can be available to Wikipedians while giving a quiz, and he keeps an eye on twenty I.R.C. chat channels, where users often trade gossip about abuses they have witnessed.
>
> ... some admins (Essjay among them) can purge text from the system, so that even the history page bears no record of its ever having been there.

Essjay didn't just step in on Justin Timberlake disputes. Discussing an entry on the term 'imprimatur', as used by Roman Catholics, Essjay championed the theological authority of *Catholicism for Dummies* – 'a text I often require for my students, and I would hang my own PhD on it's [sic] credibility.'

It wasn't his advocacy of Catholicism for Dummies or his keen interest in pop culture that brought Essjay to the attention of an online group of Wikipedia watchers. It was his user profile. It appeared too good to be true. One of the Wiki-watchers, Daniel Brandt, had been particularly suspicious of Essjay. On 26 July 2006, Brandt began a discussion thread: 'Who is Essjay? I would love to ID this guy.' A day later, he offered this view of Essjay: 'Essjay is too slick to be true. I say he's a competent, professional spook who manages several employees to help him out on Wikipedia.' A spy. A member of the secret services. A government representative. A conspiracy.

By 11 January 2007, another member of the thread had solved the mystery. Essjay was Ryan Jordan, a new employee at Wikia, a commercial enterprise. At his new employer, Jordan had this to say about himself:

I'm a 24-year-old guy from Kentucky; I grew up in Kentucky, and studied philosophy and religion at Centre College in Danville, Kentucky as well as the University of Kentucky and University of Louisville. I currently live outside Louisville with my cat, Mia.

Brandt emailed the New Yorker to let them know and a few weeks later got an answer from deputy editor, Pam McCarthy:

I want to thank you for alerting us to the issues with Essjay's profile and sharing his bio, user's page, etc., with us. We are running an editor's note laying out for our readers what happened; it is in our March 5 issue, which comes out today (The Mail, page 10). Thanks again.

The *New Yorker* editor's note ran:

> We were comfortable with the material we got from Essjay because of Wikipedia's confirmation of his work and their endorsement of him. In retrospect, we should have let our readers know that we had been unable to corroborate Essjay's identity beyond what he told us.

The note ended with a dismissive aside from Jimmy Wales, one of the founders of Wikipedia and the dominant force behind the site's growth. His view of Essjay? 'I regard it as a pseudonym and I don't really have a problem with it.' In other words, fantasy identities are fine, as long as what they write seems credible enough.

Ryan Jordan/Essjay was coming under increasing pressure to step down from Wikipedia. In his farewell note, he slung a little misspelled mud back at the *New Yorker*, writing that he was:

> ... sorry the *New Yorker* chose to print what they did about me; there seems to be a belief that I knew they were going to print it, and that is not the case. I spoke with Stacy Shiff [*sic*] for over eight hours; in that time, she asked me about a variety of subjects related to Wikipedia and I gave her much to write on. (Those who know me will know I am rarely ever brief in my comments.) That she chose to focus on two rather trivial reverts to Justin Timberlake and what my userpage said came as a complete surprise to me; it was, quite honestly, my impression that it was well known that I was not who I claimed to be, and that in the absence of any confirmation, no respectible [*sic*] publication would print it.

Given the anonymity Wikipedia offers, Jordan may still be online with a new assumed identity. I'd be surprised if he wasn't.

So, what does this say about Wikipedia? Here's what one influential blogger made of it:

> Think about it: in just a couple of years, Essjay had acquired every major position in Wikipedia's class structure, every secret power you can get on there: the ability to lock out users, the ability to 'disappear' articles, the ability to decide the fate of others in arbitration, the ability to protect articles from being suddenly changed or modified by the 'wrong' folks. He'd even gotten a paying job from the for-pay version of Wikipedia! Way to go, charlatan doucheface!
>
> Wikipedia considers the ability of anonymous or un-backed-up users to be a feature. I think it's a bug. Problem is that, as Jimmy Wales knows better than anybody, Wikipedia would be unviable as a commercial entity if it had to employ editors and fact checkers.

The Essjay case shows the extent to which that bug can be exploited for personal gain and how people, even when faced with total, utter, obvious evidence that they were bamboozled will say, 'But he was such a good editor. He did so much work. I'm going to miss him …' See *Shattered Glass* in chapter one.

And where does it leave the *New Yorker*? Here's blogger David Robinson from *Freedom to Tinker*, who when the article originally appeared argued that the magazine was more trustworthy than the online encyclopaedia:

> The *New Yorker* fell short of its own standards, and took Essjay at his word without verifying his identity or even learning his name. He had, as all con men do, a plausible-sounding story, related in this case to a putative fear of professional retribution that in hindsight sits rather uneasily with his claim that he had tenure. If the magazine hadn't broken its own rules, this wouldn't have gotten into print.
>
> But that response would be too facile … Granted that per-

fect fact checking makes for a trustworthy story; how do you know when the fact checking is perfect and when it is not? You don't. More generally, predictions are only as good as someone's ability to figure out whether or not the conditions are right to trigger the predicted outcome.

So what about this case: On the one hand, incidents like this are rare and tend to lead the fact checkers to redouble their meticulousness. On the other, the fact claims in a story that are hardest to check are often for the same reason the likeliest ones to be false. Should you trust the sometimes-imperfect fact checking that actually goes on?

My answer is yes. In the wake of this episode the *New Yorker* looks very bad (and Wikipedia only moderately so) because people regard an error in the *New Yorker* to be exceptional in a way the exact same error in Wikipedia is not. This expectations gap tells me that the *New Yorker*, warts and all, still gives people something they cannot find at Wikipedia: a greater, though conspicuously not total, degree of confidence in what they read.

But the Essjays are not the principal problem. As Wikipedia has grown, its openness has made it attractive not just to fantasists seeking to play role-playing games with reality, but to rather more serious individuals and institutions: politicians, governments and corporations.

▌Wikis as spin ▐

In 2007, a researcher called Virgil Griffith came up with a tool that allowed you to look at the internet addresses of people making Wikipedia entries and cross-reference them with the organisations that owned the address. Griffith had been inspired by tales of American politicians embellishing or erasing their entries. It soon proved to be an excellent source of embarrassment.

An entry on Wal-Mart ran: 'Wages at Wal-Mart are about

20% less than at other retail stores.' It was revised by some-one at Wal-Mart to say: 'The average wage at Wal-Mart is almost double the federal minimum wage.'

An account of the Alaskan oil spill by the oil tanker *Exxon Valdez* originally noted: 'The long-term effects of the oil spill have been studied. Thousands of animals perished immediately, the best estimates are: 250,000 sea birds, 2,800 sea otters, 300 harbor seals, 250 bald eagles, up to 22 orcas, and billions of salmon and herring eggs.' This was deleted and instead an entry posted from an Exxon Mobil address read: 'Studies conducted by hundreds of scientists have confirmed that there has been no long-term severe impact to the Prince William Sound ecosystem.'

Politicians from the Hong Kong Chief Executive, Donald Tsang, through to Australia's John Howard have been found tampering with their own Wikipedia entries, for goodness' sakes.

To give you an example of how quickly information can make it on to Wikipedia, take the case of one-time British newspaper editor, Rosie Boycott. Boycott was one of the 'celebrity' contestants on a reality cooking show, *Hell's Kitchen*. She was also the first to be voted off. Nine minutes after her early departure from the programme, the exit was already recorded at the bottom of her Wikipedia entry. So far, so trivial.

The information gathered and disseminated by open sites like Wikipedia leaves them open to abuse, but it has also allowed material to be created at a phenomenal rate. If that material comes with a caveat, isn't that the case for every-thing we read? If you really want to rely on information to make an argument, shouldn't you check it?

The 'wiki' part of Wikipedia is what gives it quantity and potentially limits its quality. The calculation is that the sheer breadth of information covered makes up for problems over lack of depth. But wikis – websites where people can contribute and collaborate online – are increasingly the way we work. This book was written online via a collaborative document on Google.

They also offer a way for information to be placed in the public domain and analysed. Take a website for whistle-blowers, Wikileaks. In 2007, it published a spreadsheet purporting to list all US military equipment deployed in Afghanistan. In the old days of journalism this would have been scanned to produce a story, or probably a series of stories, with the original document hidden from view. On Wikileaks the spreadsheet is downloadable and the site has also analysed it to approximate costs for the equipment deployed and what the kit in theatre is used for. Anyone can take the data forward. The pages list suggested tasks that anyone with the time, energy and ability can apply them-selves to. The trust issue remains in the background. Is this a genuine list? We don't know, but its presence online means military analysts can see it directly and debate its authentic-ity while in possession of as full a version of the facts as any one of us. It also makes a nice informational gift to foreign and hostile powers. And we're back to trust.

Wikis are interesting, but their content suggests that, left to their own devices, people use information sharing for social purposes to an extent that dwarfs purely political or intellectual motivations.

▮ Technology trust tools ▮

Researchers at the University of California have actually tried to measure the trustworthiness of Wikipedia entries. First they work out the reputation of the author. How do they do that?

We compute the reputation of Wikipedia authors according to how long their contributions last in the Wikipedia. Specifically, authors whose contributions are preserved, or built-upon, gain reputation; authors whose contributions are undone lose reputation.

Then they apply some algorithms to compute the trust value of each word of each revision on Wikipedia. What this shows is not knowledge you can trust, but which words are most contested – be they numbers, adjectives or nouns. Algorithms are rigid, but the language on which we apply them is elastic – not endlessly stretchy, but pliable enough to prevent us nailing things down with the finality that social scientists would like.

I've focused on wikis here, but the same issues face the other major entrant into the media stakes: the search engine. Old media's biggest competitor is not the blogs and podcasts and wikis of the world, it's the search engines. Of the early entrants into the search engine 'space' only Yahoo! and Google have risen to ubiquity – it's naturally a monopoly business. Google is so much a part of the fabric of our lives that it's a powerful and much-used verb.

As a new company founded on a wave of messianic hopes for the transforming power of information technology, Google brought enthusiasm and energy to a field unencumbered by the restrictions and protections of law. Instead it had a simple and unofficial corporate motto to emphasise its very uncorporateness: 'Don't be evil.'

The founders included this statement of intent when they floated the company:

> Our intense and enduring interest was to objectively help people find information efficiently. We also believed that searching and organizing all the world's information was an unusually important task that should be carried out by a company that is trustworthy and interested in the public good. We believe a well functioning society should have abundant, free and un-

biased access to high quality information. Google therefore has a responsibility to the world.

Google users trust our systems to help them with important decisions: medical, financial and many others. Our search results are the best we know how to produce. They are unbiased and objective, and we do not accept payment for them or for inclusion or more frequent updating. We also display advertising, which we work hard to make relevant, and we label it clearly.

This is similar to a well-run newspaper, where the advertisements are clear and the articles are not influenced by the advertisers' payments. We believe it is important for everyone to have access to the best information and research, not only to the information people pay for you to see.

Noble words from a young and minted organisation. But with success, circumstances have changed. Google does business with China. Its founders are billionaires, their private jets barely distinguishable from the private jets of other billionaires.

▌ Citizen journalism ▐

For a while there it looked as if online technologies might be the answer to news's credibility and commercial problems. Blogging offered a route out of the traditional reliance on 'mainstream media'. Perhaps it could break free of the patterns of news reporting?

A month after witnessing 9/11 from his apartment, technology writer Chris Allbritton found himself out of a job. The admired but unprofitable digital journalism offering that he'd been working on was shut down. Before his online experience, Allbritton, a graduate of Columbia University's prestigious School of Journalism, had worked for both the Associated Press and the *New York Daily News*, so he was hardly an ingénue.

Allbritton set himself up as a foreign correspondent and in July 2002 headed off to northern Iraq. That October, as the build-up to war continued, he decided to try to send himself back to report from the country using blog posts. The title of his blog? *Back-to-iraq.com* or B2I, as it quickly became known. He had an online commercial ambition: his journalistic enterprise would be paid for by donations. Starting out, he was pretty optimistic about the possibilities:

> I'm just going to be the first part of a wave of independent jour- nalists using their blogs not merely as a personal site or a parallel to their professional life, but the main distribution channel for their work, with funds raised from readers such as yourselves.

The competition for funding was tough. Allbritton, seeking money to produce independent reportage from Iraq and with his story splashed across the mainstream media, found himself getting less cash than a woman asking for donations for breast implants. He was lumped into the same category as an equally enterprising TV producer who launched an online campaign to pay off her credit card debts. Still, he assured readers: 'rather than bailing out some 20-something who got herself into a mess through conspicuous consump- tion, you'll be supporting independent journalism and an adventure.'

It took six months for 300 or so donors to come up with the few thousand dollars needed to send him on his way. Allbritton's enthusiasm was undimmed. Arriving in Turkey in March, as the invasion of Iraq had got under way, he was keen to get out and report:

> [F]or the first time in my thirteen years as a journalist, I'm able to practice journalism with only one responsibility – to the readers. No editors to impress, no advertisers to stroke, no colleagues to compete against.

His first posts from inside Iraq were filed in April. Readers commenting weren't always polite. 'I don't think Chris has the insight or background to offer real reporting,' wrote someone called Amy, '… the entries simply detail his arrogant adventure.' Another reader wanted pictures, adding: 'you could be doing some creative writing from Starbucks for all we know. Please show me different.' But the audience was, for the most part, a coalition of the willing. 'You have redefined "extreme" reporting,' wrote a fan, 'I anxiously await your next entry, like a daily reality fix.'

Altogether Allbritton managed just over a fortnight in Iraq, finally making it to Baghdad before his money ran out and he had to return to New York. On its best day, his site had attracted over 20,000 visitors. Not everyone thought the experiment had worked:

> After what I gather looks to be somewhere in the region of what, four or five months preparation to get this trip off the ground, you spend twenty days in Iraq, missed the conflict by a matter of days and are already back in New York.
>
> As a vehicle to cover news stories, blogging is far too slow in terms of getting the finance together to fund the trip.

The mainstream media were more enthusiastic. *Business-Week* magazine suggested his trip could break the mould on reporting:

> Allbritton's story hints at a new business model that could remake the lesser tiers of the media world. Call it pay-to-read journalism. Reporters, individually or in groups, could use the Net to raise money directly from readers interested in specific stories or journalistic styles.

Later that year another blogging journalist was attempting to get readers to pay for him to cover an event, this time a political convention in the US. Allbritton noted on his blog:

'I may have been the first, I certainly hope I'm not the last to do this kind of reader-funded reporting.' Fundraising began for the next trip.

By May 2004 he was ready to return, but with a rather less ambitious project than before:

> ... this endeavour can't be the not-for-profit jaunt the last trip was. Then, I specifically rejected freelance assignments from magazines so I could concentrate on pure blogging. I can't do that this time, as the money raised from this fund-raising call, as well as my own savings, will go for the initial costs of establishing a presence in Baghdad.

And when he did move to Baghdad a month later, Allbritton faced a backlash from some readers, forcing him to admit that:

> Reader donations don't really cover the approximately $4,000/month burn rate for driver, housing and fixer. I like working freelance as well, and I want to advance my career. This may strike some of you as 'selling out' but I've been clear about my intentions since I started raising funds again ...

Although many were understanding, one begged to differ:

> You're clearly compromising your stated intent to be an independent voice ... You're not a hero simply because you are there and going through the steps to further your journalism career – you solicited a significant amount of money from readers and you have a responsibility to them that is equal or greater than the other publications that you're writing for.

To which Allbritton responded:

> Iraq is a completely different environment from during the war. Ironically, it's actually more difficult to work here than it

was then. And compromising my independence is a necessary, well, compromise to ensure safety.

That compromise meant working with the same media outlets his backers so disdained. Later that month, favourably reviewing a report from the *Washington Post*, Allbritton confronted some of the comfortable prejudices of his own readership:

> [W]hy is there such a widespread feeling that the media, as it's all lumped together sometimes, is worthless? Two recent comments brought this question to the fore for me:
>
> 'Good to read an impartial view of what's afoot over there, as I don't believe a word of the news most of the time. Thanks.' – kat
>
> 'Its good to see what is actually going on in iraq and not follow the spoon fed media of western society.' – Solaris. M.K.A.
>
> ... I have to ask these two commenters – who are just being used as examples only – well, why not?
>
> I'm not trying to pick a fight, but this is a question that has puzzled me since the beginning. I mean, I'm not impartial; I've revealed my anti-war feelings from the get-go. So why is B2I considered more credible than others? Other journalists are on the ground here, too, so it's not just authority by way of location.

One commenter agreed: 'Rather than blaming the media for its failures to educate us, what have we been doing to educate ourselves? Why should the media be shouldered with the entire burden?'

And another pointed to the polarised anti-war community that supported B2I: 'People like to feel they are part of a community, get the news from a source that complies with their own feelings on a subject as apparent by the posting here ... The problem with the news is the masses it serves, not the masters. WE want a few points of information to squeeze into our busy day. That's what WE get.'

Although he left Baghdad for Beirut, Allbritton remained a poster-boy for online, independent journalism. When Allbritton was quoted as an example by one of the genre's most powerful advocates, New York journalism professor Jay Rosen, Allbritton posted this dismissive postscript to the whole adventure:

> Opinion and argument is the currency of the blogosphere, not reporting – a statement that seems rather self-evident if you spend any time on the Internet.
>
> When I started *Back-to-Iraq*, almost five years ago, I was hopeful that my brand of online journalism, supported by the public, would take off. That's not been the case. Why? Because doing journalism is expensive.
>
> … I stopped getting donations long ago – I got kind of bored by the hustle required – and I support myself by free-lancing.
>
> … So, blog away, but please leave me out of the lists showing bloggers doing journalism.

The blog, where one reporter could strike out alone, turns out not to be the future of journalism. Not for want of trying, though.

▌ Network effects ▐

The old certainties of news have been swept away by the internet. Pardon?

For years journalists thought, rather sensibly, that what made stories popular was their ability to appeal to large numbers of people. A popular story was, by definition, a good one. A news story's popularity was explained entirely in terms of its inherent qualities.

The editors who could identify these qualities most consistently published the most popular stories and were the best journalists. So far, so obvious. Yet, somehow, so not right. Because they seemed to get it wrong a lot. Surveys showed that the stories editors liked weren't the ones the public rated. And when journalism moved online, webpages could keep a precise track of exactly how many times a story was viewed, for how long, and by whom. One of the longest running and most popular stories on the BBC website – generating millions of hits – featured a man who had been caught having sex with his goat. In a name-and-shame operation, the local magistrates had made the guy 'marry' the goat.

The piece had originally been carried in a small publication in southern Sudan, the *Juba Post*. A Brit, Tom Rhodes, edited it. His paper had a website but Rhodes didn't bother to post it.

In his capacity as editor of the *Juba Post*, Rhodes had been what marketing people call an early adopter. But his publication's limited circulation wasn't enough to give the story international currency. For that the story needed to get to the BBC website. That was when the audience took it on themselves to pass it on.

The *Juba Post* and the BBC both rely on professional journalists to put their pages together, offline and on. But sites like Google News build a front page just by using an algorithm. They aggregate stuff that's getting attention – the idea ought to be that you aggregate the professional judgements of journalists everywhere and get some kind of crowd-sourced wisdom. The reality is that many sites just post agency copy to keep their rankings and so Google News becomes a vast dumping ground for wire service copy, running under nearly identical headlines from Nantucket to New Delhi.

Google News didn't really provide the clue as to how popularity worked. It took social media sites to do that.

Digg allowed members to vote on their favourite bits of the internet and built its front page accordingly. More active members were rewarded with more influence.

Anything could be included – from blogs to the *Daily Telegraph* or the *Los Angeles Times*.

Here's how it works, explained by David Cohn, a young journalism graduate in the US, known on Digg as DigiDave:

> Every time one of my submissions is voted onto the front page, my rank among Digg's 600,000 contributors is enhanced. As of this writing I am ranked forty-third and have become a trusted contributor, watched by more than two hundred people who are notified whenever I submit a new story, which, in turn, gives my submissions a better chance at reaching Digg's front page.

That front page is produced by people like Cohn – enthusiasts. And as he makes clear, the more people follow their recommendations, the more power the algorithm gives them, so Digg creates its own editors, called, unsurprisingly, Diggers. The top Diggers are listed on the site and between them they create about half the front page.

So is the digitally democratic system more trustworthy? Well, here's the rub. With power as a Digger comes the temptation to be paid for using it. Diggs generate traffic. On a modest level Cohn is free to recommend his own writing, thereby bringing his own audience of several thousand to any online publication he writes for. There's no law against self-promotion. And if his work isn't up to standard his fellow recommenders are free to bury it – the Digg equivalent of a thumbs down.

Besides self-promotion, you could also be paid to Digg things. Digg doesn't want you to and if they find out you're cheating you're off the system. But what's to lose? A reporter caught cheating could have his career ended. A Digger risks only removal from the platform.

Digg could change the mathematics that gave Diggers their power, but in an online community this only generates other online communities devoted to finding their way around such changes. So a new editorial game, played partly in public partly in private, replaces an old one that took place with no participation whatsoever. The private ethics of trust patrolled by fellow professionals gives way to the self-policing public.

If we're still no nearer a formula, it may at least be possible to see some of the mechanisms by which stories become popular. And this is where sociologist Duncan Watts comes in.

Watts carried out an online experiment with music. Thousands of users signed up to a website to access free music. Watts and his team let them listen, download and rate tracks by unknown bands. All the bands started at zero. One user group saw only the artists and their songs; another saw the most popular downloads. This group was split into lots of mini-groups.

Now according to the 'inherent qualities' argument the same tunes should have been popular with the people who just saw the titles and with the people who saw the number of downloads. Not just that, but the most downloaded should be pretty much the same across every mini-group that could see the rankings.

It didn't turn out like that. While quality did play some part in a song's success – establishing a kind of threshold – the download figures skewed people's choices. That means a changing group of early adopters made success in music fundamentally unpredictable. Think about how that works in news with stories. The Sudanese goat is brought up to threshold by being reported in the *Juba Post*. But how does it get wider currency? An agency reporter or another paper picks it up, then another, till finally it appears on one of the biggest online sites, the BBC and – by virtue of making the most-emailed list – it continues to have a half-life as a curiosity even though it long ago stopped being news.

Network effects describe the process by which a technology's attractiveness increases with the number of people using it – like telephones. When only two people have them, owning one has limited value. When 2 billion have them, it's a necessity.

So if there is an unpredictability and randomness in the kinds of stories that 'capture the public imagination', what about quality? The songs Watts catalogued still had to conform to the basic values we've come to expect from pop or rock. It wasn't simply noise that was being downloaded.

So, what are the formulas that news producers use?

Think of a traditional news broadcast, an old fashioned recipe now, half a century in the making. The broadcast is live, so too are some of the reporters but the bulk of the time is filled with material that has been pre-recorded and pre-edited.

The running time, depending on adverts, could be as little as 21 minutes with two commercial breaks for a US network, or an uninterrupted half hour for a public service broadcaster like the BBC. Into this bucket of time news is poured until the brim is reached – full, no more.

Put like that, there can be few things as daunting as sitting down at the beginning of the day to fill that time. The reality is a little more straightforward. Programmes are templated. The introduction by the main anchor can run between fifteen and 30 seconds. The pieces are similarly slotted. The template can be made to run all the way to time exactly, so that a programme might be half a dozen pieces, a couple of lives and a feature report, or a sports round-up, or the weather.

Editorial judgement consists of the ordering of stories and their delivery, but mostly it consists of filling the bucket, because the bucket can never go empty or be left half full. There are notable exceptions. A friend once read a local radio bulletin whose template ended, 'Scottish news, if any'.

Just because there's a formula doesn't mean there isn't skill or judgement involved. A sonnet has a set of rules too and no one said that doesn't mean poetry. But the rules of rhyme and metre are explicit; a sonnet wears its rules in its fourteen lines – the media is less transparent. And if you don't know the formula it's hard to question it and when mistakes are made, harder still to understand them. Instead of admitting that this is all we can give you, a programme running order says that this is all there is. Whatever their relative importance from one day to the next, headlines are delivered with the same sense of urgency.

Journalists know this but they can't escape it. The programme formula and the stilted language in which it is delivered has spawned everything from sketch show parodies, like *The Day Today*, to actual comedy news programmes like Jon Stewart's *The Daily Show*. *The Daily Show* is made by Comedy Central, but is rebroadcast on CNN International, thereby completing a self-referential cycle in which TV news all but disappears up its own orifice.

Journalism is just the showerhead, it's up to audiences to determine the power and the temperature, and how long – if at all – to spend beneath the flow.

Formulas aren't just used in TV news. One of the most formulaic types of news is agency copy. To give you an example, in June 2002, Associated Press reporter Chris Newton filed a piece headed 'New Technology For Catching Liars'.

'The world is becoming a trickier place for people who tell lies,' he began, 'even little white ones.' It reviewed some new lie detection equipment being tested in labs. The piece also considered the legal implications of rolling out such kit.

Thomas Jakes, president of People for Civil Rights, was not impressed: 'Voices can shake because people are scared about being interrogated by police ... This technology is nothing but a way to scare people.'

Justin Hammerstein, a civil liberties attorney in New York, was less forthright: 'As long as no one was being arrested or detained solely on the basis of the test, there is no law against scanning someone's face with a device ... You could use the device to subject someone to greater scrutiny in a physical search or background check, and it would be hard to argue that it is illegal.'

Last word in the story went to Dale Jenang, a sociologist and philosophy researcher at the University of California, Berkeley: 'We should try to avoid a society where suspicion is based on a machine and not on evidence. Guilt and innocence are too important to leave to a machine.'

Jakes, Hammerstein and Jenang were not the only people Newton quoted in the story. But they were the only ones who appeared to be – well – made up. There didn't seem to be a People for Civil Rights either. Not that anyone checked at the time. Newton's talent for invention finally came to light when a *New York Times* reporter tried to follow up a story on crime statistics. Newton had got a leak of some figures ahead of time. His piece quoted two experts, Ralph Myers from Stanford University, and Bruce Fenmore from Chicago's Institute for Crime and Punishment. Stanford University exists although Ralph didn't, but the Institute for Crime and Punishment appeared to be as much a work of fiction as its name suggested.

A little over a week after the story ran, Newton was fired. AP sent out a correction and went through his back catalogue looking for other imaginary experts.

In 2000, they found three stories where people quoted couldn't be tracked down. By 2001 there were 22. And when they finally caught him in September 2002 the total was up to 40, with five coming in August. There was obviously a rhythm to invention.

Newton was unwilling to admit they were phoney, as the AP noted in its usual tightly written, scrupulous way:

> Before his dismissal, Newton was asked about questionable material in a number of his stories. He maintained that the experts in those stories were real and accurately quoted, but was unwilling or unable to provide proof of their authenticity.

The quotes concocted by Newton probably went undetected for so long because they were so banal. They fitted the formula. Point, counterpoint; view, counter-view. They didn't appear to be self-serving – unless they allowed him time to put his feet up in the office. They were hardly the stuff of award-winning journalism. They might even have been a small act of rebellion against the rigid impersonal style of wire service journalism. If they were, it was a misplaced rebellion.

It's not the medium that is trusted. It's the message.

CHAPTER FIVE

And Here is the News

All news, whether it appears on the front page of the *Sun* or BBC's *Newsnight*, is created, produced and manufactured. All news involves some form of artifice. A chain is as strong as its weakest link and news is as trustworthy as the least trustworthy element involved in its production.

But most people would agree that there is a material difference between inserting a cutaway shot of a nodding reporter into an interview and fabricating the interview altogether. This is a line, however, that the news media has never really been too fussed about crossing.

In 1926, aged 44, Silas Bent, who had been a newspaperman, journalism professor and PR man, began an essay titled 'Journalism and Morality'. He kicked it off with an example of professional practice from the beginning of his career. Bent's first reporting job, aged eighteen, was on the *Louisville Herald* in Kentucky, but by 21 he was on the staff of the altogether grander *St Louis Post-Dispatch*, the paper whose foundation had been the making of Joseph Pulitzer (he of the journalism prizes).

Bent was reporting on a scandal of the time – an elopement between a middle-aged woman and a millionaire cosmetics manufacturer. The woman had a grown-up daughter, and Bent was calling at the family home. Or, more accurately, pulling the doorbell off in his attempts to attract attention. His paper had reported the affair but it had no hard evidence or court case to back it up. Bent's job was to stand up what had already appeared and move the story forward.

He had all but abandoned his mission when a messenger arrived with a telegram. Mistaking Bent for a friend of the family, he asked him to sign for it. Bent signed with a fake name, pocketed the message and made good his escape. The telegram revealed the location of the eloped couple.

Bent had actually committed a felony, but he was not concerned:

> The anxiety behind this telegram did not at all concern me, nor was I concerned at having stolen it. As the child of God-fearing parents I think I may say I had a strict sense of private property rights: I would not have pilfered ten cents or ten dollars. But my conscience was wholly untroubled about the message, because I had done the conventional thing ... I was exultant, not ashamed ...

The eloped couple left their hideaway immediately and Bent was dispatched to meet them halfway. Thereafter his editors expected him to deliver the goods. Since then, of course, journalism has evolved in both professionalism and seriousness. There are now libraries written about journalism ethics, regulatory bodies that preside over hearings about journalists' infractions, university courses designed to teach would-be journalists and experienced hacks alike the intricacies of the professional code.

So how much have things really changed in the last four score or so years? Here's a story from the beginning of a journalistic career that began about 90 years after Bent's. It's about a young producer looking to get his first story on the US network news. Competition to get a piece on the evening news was intense. Yarns were pitched to the desk and sold to the fishbowl. To get an ordinary news story in front of millions of Americans required political manoeuvring and expert timing.

This young hack found one he could deliver – delinquent youths stealing cars and joyriding around the winding streets of a poor housing project. But the piece needed pictures – of drag racing youngsters in hot cars – and there was no guaranteeing when that might happen.

Problem was, the young producer could have the cameras and crew for one night only. So, he went to a local bar and asked how one might see such races. A couple of youngsters knew the answers, or claimed to, and he did a deal – if they could let the people responsible know when the camera crew was around, they would be paid. The producer was careful. No one was to be asked to steal cars or do anything they wouldn't otherwise be doing. They were just to be sent a message: that there would be a television crew around filming on a particular evening.

That particular evening came around quickly and the first thing the producer and his team did was to interview the people who lived on the project about the problems caused by the racers. It was important to do these interviews first, because afterwards – if there was an afterwards – they couldn't hang around.

In the evening, they returned to film. Several stolen cars were in action, performing gyratory handbrake turns, wheels smoking, speeding round narrow streets. There were no police to be seen. As the cars raced around the precincts, spectators gathered and the young producer realised it was quite possible that the drivers might crash and kill themselves, or lose control and plough into the sidewalks, killing people who'd come out to watch. Still, there was no denying it – this was spectacular footage.

Before leaving, the producer paid the young men who had 'facilitated' the piece. That was the description on the expense form: 'facility fee'. For the producer it was a reporting triumph. The story made the evening news. The producer saw his name roll through the credits as he sat in a New York apartment looking out over Washington Square and the Empire State, a warm champagne fuzz flushing his cheeks.

For the people of the housing project, it was just another night. Some had had their cars stolen and run into the ground. Luckily, no one had been injured. No one had been paid to commit a crime. In the end, the police ended up doing something about a problem they'd avoided. The project's troubled youth had to find a new way to interrupt their boredom. And the young producer learned a valuable lesson: the importance of being lucky. And that there might be such a thing as too good to be true.

No prizes for guessing the identity of the producer. That would be me, a can-do kind of guy.

When you consider how this stuff is put together, it shouldn't be asking too much of people to bring a certain amount of scepticism to the table when they think about the media. That's as it should be. The best way is to know what you're dealing with, know your enemy as it were. Take the clock apart and put it back together again.

◗▌ The news cycle ▐◖

Imagine a Bond-style gathering of international villains, male, in early middle age, meeting in secretive luxury and conspiring to promote certain causes and suppress others. Surprisingly, this is pretty much how the news agenda is set on a daily basis. Apart from the luxury bit.

If you asked editors, they certainly wouldn't think of themselves as serving an agenda. The more pragmatic and world-weary would think of their mission as servicing what American newspapers charmingly term the 'news hole'. Every day editors have to fill the hole. Some have Grand Canyon-sized holes to fill into which every story may be flung, others have petite holes the size of a plot in a pet cemetery.

Into these holes, stories are poured. Some will come from agencies like Reuters and the Associated Press, which news organisations subscribe to. Others will be running stories like court cases or politics; still others will come from within the news organisation itself.

Think how easy it would be to build your own television news bulletin. Every night you would carry a story from Westminster on the latest political shenanigans. Every night you would do one very big international story – a plane crash, a hurricane, the latest news from the Middle East using agency pictures. America is always good for one story, be it celebrity news or the latest from the White House. Then you might have a health/business/education/crime/showbiz story. None of it can be longer than two or three minutes. Shuffle the order and put in some sports headlines and you're halfway to having a programme.

That short outline is intended to give some idea of the juggling that goes on behind the rather haughty expression 'editorial judgement'. The hole needs filling. Resources determine the amount of coverage you're able to provide. This is the frame in which daily decision-making on news takes place – the things that are assumed before you even begin to look at the actual story content. What is the top line? The content is actually the last part of the editorial selection process.

▮▮ Why do all news outlets cover the same story at the same time? ▮▮

The answer has less to do with the intrinsic values of the stories themselves, and the bias of the people who select and report them, and more to do with the market. To start to answer the questions, let's look at newspapers. They compete on price, availability (street sellers at train stations), physical quality (e.g. colour photos, graphics quality) and promotions (giveaways or advertising). Why do they spectacularly fail to compete sometimes on story selection?

It's all about product positioning. Back in 1929, an economist called Harold Hotelling first put forward a rationale under which companies were likely to make their products as similar as possible. Hotelling's law predicts that on a street with two shops, both will put themselves bang in the middle, carving up the households between them.

The people living on the street would find life easier if the two shops put themselves a quarter of the way from each end of the street. But neither shop is going to do that because the other could shift and capture over half the market. If you apply that positioning to news outlets, then you should be able to position yourself on both story treatment and story selection.

When it comes to stories, that isn't always the case. A bewildered audience confronted with the same story on radio, TV, online and in print is left wondering if there is some kind of herd instinct that drives journalists towards the identical tale, leaving their collective hoof prints on whoever or whatever dares to stand in their way. And when you look back over media coverage from the sinking of the *Titanic* to Madeleine McCann's disappearance, the answer seems probably, yes – but it's not instinct but market dynamics that are driving the stampede.

So what makes big stories bigger? Think of them as speculative bubbles in the news market and the answers are simple. Imagine you are a news editor and have to choose your main story. You also have to choose the amount of space you want to give it and the amount of resources you will commit to it. Where will you commit your reporters? Spread them thinly across a range of stories? Or put them on what you think is the top story? It's a no-brainer.

And what makes you think a story is the lead? The competitive environment (shaped by other journalists) and your professional judgement (shared with other journalists). The advantage of going with a story already being run by rivals is obvious. The costs of retelling it are almost non-existent – they've done the work for you. With only a modest investment of reporting time and energy, you can acquire an incremental fact or comment and compete successfully or – if the new information you gather moves the story on sufficiently – scoop them completely.

Go against the pack – and get it wrong – and you risk flying in the face of the judgement of your peers. As John Maynard Keynes once wrote, '[I]t is better for reputation to fail conventionally than to succeed unconventionally'. So there's safety in numbers. In case you wonder just how strong this force is, when I worked at CBS News, the top editorial execs slavishly followed the *New York Times* when making a judgement about what made a foreign story. If you offered up a story in anticipation of the *New York Times*, this was evidence of precipitate – not superior – judgement. So producers in the field would co-operate with *Times* reporters and wait to pitch feature stories to coincide with their appearance in the newspaper of record.

Now, too, online news sites can see what stories are being read and skew their resources accordingly. In the case of Madeleine McCann, the Associated Press – one of the biggest news organisations in the world – moved reporters from covering a summit of European leaders to a press conference on the story of a missing toddler.

This movement of resources is what economists call positive feedback. When all these factors come together, you have the 'big story' phenomenon. Big stories aren't as frequent as you'd think, though. I once worked on a programme with just that title – *The Big Story* – that had been sold to the network on the promise of doing – yes, you guessed it – the big story of the week. We quickly discovered that there really wasn't one as often as the network pitch had indicated, so the programme fell back into a standard current affairs formula.

The costs of operating as 'newsgatherer of first resort', going out and finding stuff out, outweigh the benefits of a big running story, since everyone can pitch in and find an angle. But where they do provide an advantage in the market is at times when no story consensus exists. That's when you see the power of a paper like the *Daily Mail* – Britain's mid-market leader, and the country's second most-read paper – on other news organisations, particularly broadcasters.

Some stories push all news organisations in the same direction. Take the British government's infamous dossier to make the case for war with Iraq. The dossier contained the claim that Saddam Hussein possessed chemical or biological weapons that could be deployed within 45 minutes.

That was the disputed claim that brought the British government and the BBC to blows at the Hutton Inquiry. From that inquiry you'd have thought that everyone swallowed the claim whole. Actually, this is how the dossier was reported:

- The dossier doesn't contain many surprises – *BBC News*
- Iraq Dossier Fails To Persuade – *Aberdeen Press & Journal*
- Nothing new in Saddam's stockpile of evil weapons – *Birmingham Post*
- The dossier that answers nothing – *Daily Mail*
- No, he cannot threaten London or New York – Jane Corbin, *Daily Mail*
- PM's Dossier 'Not Enough' – *Daily Star*
- He's Got 'Em ... Let's Get Him – *Sun*

- This is not a dossier but an act of desperation – Simon Jenkins, *The Times*

Although everyone carried the story, the coverage reflected not just the British government's position but also a certain healthy scepticism. The list illustrates that the British news media tends to differentiate on story treatment.

But the question remains – somewhere in news land an editor has to make a judgement about the value of a story. How do they do that? The answer has just as much to do with economics as it does with 'impact'.

▌ What are the most valuable stories? ▌

Stories aren't valuable. Readers, viewers and listeners are. How valuable? Advertisers, not journalists, decide on that.

Television advertisers tend to want to reach young people between the ages of 18–34. So, in a competitive environment where do you position yourself to get your audience? Well, in the days of only a few channels, television executives would look at the available audience and schedule accordingly. News would invariably find itself pushed out to the edge of primetime, either at the beginning or the end. The television audience rises in the course of the evening, as does its demographic. Wealthy professionals, for example, are not usually home by six.

Invariably too it would face counter-scheduling. In the United States, for example, the three evening newscasts occupy exactly the same time slots. It makes sense to take your news pain at the same time.

So you also face the available audience. On conventional, scheduled TV, programmes 'inherit' audiences from programmes that went before them. They are judged by how well they retain or build those audiences. Advertisers will also be interested in breaking down the demographic composition of viewing figures. A million school children will be worth less to car advertisers than a million forty-some-things. Niche subscription channels are in a different position.

For newspapers, the bargain is different. Traditionally, they relied on advertising and subscription. A newspaper charging £1 a copy and selling a quarter of a million copies a day will bring in nearly £80 million a year. You can see why newspaper editors are loath to stop charging. But in recent years all the growth has been in free, advertising-funded newspapers.

A look at the London evening market will give you some idea of the problems newspapers face. DMGT's *Evening Standard* was for many years the only evening paper remaining in the capital. From the mid-2000s, it faced competition from a Murdoch free sheet, the *London Paper*. DMGT introduced its own free sheet, *London Lite*, and raised the price of the *Standard*, emphasising its 'quality'. The *Standard* lost a lot of readers but those it kept were paying more. *London Lite* was positioned as a much more tabloid offering, leaving the *London Paper* in the middle.

The free sheets were distributed by street vendors. The giveaways also gnawed at the London readership of the tabloids. The *Sun* found itself having to cut its cover price and use the same street vendors to maintain its market share. Both the free sheets on offer were well resourced enough in terms of content provision, so the battle became less about stories and more about distribution, marketing and positioning.

By way of example, the free sheets actually stopped running stories on their front pages and gave them over to ads, a perfect indication of the value of stories in a market where content resources are relatively equal.

In Britain, the *Independent*, which is comparatively poorly resourced in content and newsgathering terms, positions itself as a 'viewspaper', and runs against the editorial grain of competition. Again, this is a perfectly rational resource-based decision. If you can't challenge on depth and breadth of coverage, find another point of difference. The *Independent* is engaging in a form of editorial arbitrage.

▌ Who decides what's news? Manufacturing the news vs. newsgathering ▐

[I]t is charged by the public against the press that its dominating interest is in sex and crime. I think this is to misread motives. The dominating interest of the press seems so often to be in sex and crime because sex and crime ... so often furnish the best story. For here, compact and vivid, is the personal fight with the well-identified antagonists and the stage set for suspense.

That was American writer, Charles Merz, asking rather grandly what made a front page lead back in the 1920s. A year after he wrote that, the *New York Daily Mirror*, a tabloid of the most shameless variety – and lacking a decent crime story – decided to investigate an unresolved double murder in which a minister and a lady from his choir had been found dead together.

The *Mirror* said there was new evidence in the case and its efforts led to the minister's widow being brought to trial. Sixty telegraph wires were laid on outside the courtroom and nearly 200 reporters covered the case (over a dozen of them from the lofty *New York Times*). Each day the trial ran, half a million words went out over the telegraph wires.

A murder trial was a show, a newspaper just the impresario. As a contemporary journalist wrote:

In some form and at some point the element of suspense enters into every great news story: suspense as to the story's end in life or death, in victory or defeat, in honour or demotion … The best news story, like the most successful fiction in the magazines, leaves its reader counting hours for the next edition.

Although our appetite for crime is no longer at the fever pitch level of the 1920s, crime stories still run to recognisable patterns. Take a non-domestic murder, for example. How does it get dramatised? First, it is particularised. Although the police solve crimes by looking for patterns that relate to previous investigations, journalists sell stories by emphasising their uniqueness and points of difference. Reporters would look to seize on a peculiarity in the case and 'identify' the murderer, for example 'the Boston strangler'. To keep the story alive, there's some scope to run with the idea of 'a community in fear'. Where will the killer strike next?

Then, unless the murderer obliges by striking again – and in the absence of an arrest – coverage can move on to question police competence as 'the investigation drags'. The police, anticipating such a predictable turn of events, will have held back some detail of the crime that can then run as 'new lead in hunt for killer'. And so it goes …

▮ Bad news ▮

Journalists get a pasting for always valuing 'bad' news, but invariably they are presenting information because they want people to do something. In the case of headlines, for example, what they want people to do is just read the whole story.

When it comes to information about public affairs, what gets people going – good news or bad? In the middle of the Second World War, a couple of American psychologists, Floyd Allport and Milton Lepkin, tested headlines about US victories and US setbacks on the public. Counter to everything you assumed about propaganda, this is what they found:

> Generally speaking, the worse the news reported in a headline, the greater its morale value and, conversely, the better the news, the smaller the stimulus to war participation.

They actually criticised newspapers for putting too 'rosy' a complexion on war news because it would undermine morale by disengaging the public. The Red Cross, for example, noted that blood donations dropped after good news. They found that all war news stimulated a desire by the public to get behind the war effort – but really bad news in particular. Among Allport and Lepkin's top morale-boosting headlines:

- Americans Lose 5 Troopships In African Occupation
- 3 US Heavy Cruisers Sunk By Japs
- Major Attack On Guadalcanal Opened By Japan

Not exactly what the authorities might have imagined would be good publicity. But it's basic stuff about adversity driving community cohesion. A common enemy brings us together closer, quicker.

As Nazi propaganda chief Joseph Goebbels discovered after the defeat at Stalingrad, it became easier to mobilise people as the level of threat increased. It's not a very palatable lesson.

▌ Disaster coverage ▐

In 2006, Carma International, a media monitoring company that usually spends its time tracking the 'reputations' of major corporations, turned its attention instead to disaster coverage.

What drove reporting of big humanitarian disasters? They chose to study six: Hurricanes Stanley and Katrina; earthquakes that destroyed the Iranian city of Bam and one that devastated communities in Kashmir; the Asian Tsunami; and the ongoing humanitarian crisis in Darfur.

Unsurprisingly, death toll didn't drive coverage. Hurricane Katrina, which generated the most reporting by far, killed and displaced the least number of people. Although the crisis in Darfur produced a death toll estimated to be in the region of a couple of hundred thousand, the Asian Tsunami produced nearly twice as much coverage. Twenty-five thousand people died in Bam, but it got about the same amount of coverage as the earthquake in Kashmir, where some 90,000 people were believed to have been killed. The two earthquakes and Hurricane Stanley got a tenth of the overall space in coverage of all the disasters.

So if it wasn't mortality that drove reporting, what was it? Resources and self-interest. Hurricane Katrina devastated a major US city with the best-equipped media in the world. Their immediate presence generated free media for distribution onto the world market. The hurricane also had domestic political implications for the most powerful government on the planet – the Bush administration. The hurricane also damaged oil installations in the Gulf of Mexico and the costs of repairing it all hit world insurance markets. Nearly a fifth of the coverage concentrated on the economic implications of the story.

In Darfur, a regional conflict was taking place in an oil-rich corner of Sudan that was China's main source of foreign oil. In the case of the Asian Tsunami, a disaster hit the global tourism industry, killing Western holidaymakers – 40 per cent of the coverage was about Westerners, although they made up a tiny fraction of the victims overall.

Neither the Bam nor the Kashmiri earthquakes – although they hit politically sensitive areas – held much impact for the global economy. Just 1 per cent of the coverage of the Bam earthquake took that line and not one article mentioned it with regards to Kashmir. In the case of Hurricane Stanley – which you're probably struggling to recall since it mostly struck Guatemala – there were neither sufficient deaths nor any economic consequences much beyond the communities affected, so again, there was no coverage.

Similarly, disasters could generate a kind of backslapping, with the media lavishing praise on their audience. 'The British public should be feeling a little better about itself this morning', wrote the *Sunday Times* about Tsunami donations on 2 January 2005. The next day, Down Under? 'Australian donors had been among the most generous in the world. This is eclipsing anything we've seen before by a long way', trilled the *Sydney Morning Herald*.

The Carma report identified two directions that coverage took. One was to further a continuing debate (e.g. climate change), the other was to fit the disaster into the context of national interests.

For example, over half the reporting of Hurricane Katrina focused not on the problems of those affected, but on the Bush administration. What had been done? Whose career in Washington was over? How would this influence the war in Iraq? One way of widening a story is by dumping it on the doorstep of a politician. George W. Bush is a national and international figure, whose every move is covered by a permanent gang of media, the White House Press Corps. Bush played across all America. The response of the New Orleans police department played only in a submerged corner of Louisiana.

While we're here, the way this process occurs, of taking stories and then putting them into a different context, is called 'framing'. Framing isn't a word journalists use often, it comes from academics, but it's shorter than contextualise, means the same and is thus to be preferred.

To give you an example of how framing works, in September 2007, when the parents of Madeleine McCann were official suspects in the disappearance of their daughter, BBC Radio 5 Live decided to run a phone-in discussion on the theme, 'Do You Still Support the McCanns'? Given that listeners were unlikely to have any privileged information to share, they were in effect being asked if the McCanns were innocent or guilty. That question framed the discussion so controversially that the BBC ended up having to withdraw it.

This is the reason we have criminal trials, because although your freedom ultimately rests with an opinion poll sample of twelve, they are, in theory, guided by the evidence brought before them and its formal presentation in a court of law, not the scuttlebutt they hear on the grapevine.

▮ Media regulation ▮

The media, like any other business, is regulated for competition. There are other strictures too. In the US, you have to be a citizen to own TV stations, hence a certain ex-Australian's allegiance to Uncle Sam. Here in Britain, the Competition Commission keeps an eye on who owns too much of any one thing and where market influence becomes market dominance. Sometimes to buy new businesses you have to sell old things.

And who makes regulations? Well, politicians do. In newspapers, it's just ownership that's regulated. Since the 1950s, the British industry has paid for its own regulator to answer public complaints. A little rebranding exercise in the 1990s turned it from the Press Council into the Press Complaints Commission, but otherwise it answers the few thousand or so Britons who every year have reason to believe that it can provide redress for whatever ill has been visited upon them by newspapers, be it trivial or grave.

Television and radio, along with telecoms companies,

mobile phone operators and cable and satellite providers, are ruled over by Ofcom, a government-backed regulator. It doesn't always have the sharpest of teeth.

Take Item 10.3 of Ofcom's Broadcasting Code. It says: 'Products and services must not be promoted in programmes.' It's the old Chinese Wall – editorial decision-making and the selling of advertising must forever remain separate. Stories are always reported on merit. Advertising has to be paid for.

What does this mean in practice? In 2006, a regional ITV transport correspondent brought his editor an interesting story – Virgin Atlantic, a local company (well, the airport was in the region), were about to launch a new service to Dubai. By aeroplane! Time for an all-expenses-paid Virgin 72-hour press trip to the Gulf and a competition for viewers to win free Virgin flights to … Dubai! Well, you can't legislate for a coincidence like that.

Thankfully, ITV managed to retain complete editorial independence over the story – well, stories. You can't push off for three days and not bring two stories back, and it gives viewers twice the opportunity to win a fantastic holiday to Dubai. But viewers are an ungrateful lot and one of them complained to Ofcom.

True, there was a mention of the launch of Virgin's new flights and an interview with Virgin boss Sir Richard Branson in the first report, and perhaps – on reflection – ITV had probably devoted too much airtime to the Dubai features. But, news bosses claimed, this was the product of an enthusiastic reporter and a desire on the part of the producers to introduce something a little different into the programmes. Here are just a few of the plugs the reporter put in the script:

Dubai is just a seven-hour flight away with a record 100 flights a week from Gatwick and Heathrow.

British airlines are starting new routes all the time. The latest is Virgin Atlantic with its usual high profile launch.

Well they say Dubai has everything and by the looks of it, it certainly does ...

In the shopping malls you're never far away from a familiar brand. This one is home to 300 shops and there are plenty more. In the old part of town, the souks and the famous gold markets offer good bargains.

It's all just a seven-hour flight away and with low crime rates, it's one of the safest places to visit ...

The flights take just seven hours and there are 84 a week from Heathrow and Gatwick.

... If it's the weather, security and a rest you're after, it's worth a visit.

Ofcom fined ITV nothing for advertising Virgin's services. It just cost them a dressing down. Cases like this make you wonder what regulation is really for – and also what happens to companies who offer freebies to journalists. Virgin weren't even ticked off for offering the trip in the first place.

Which raises the question, who regulates the journalists themselves and keeps them honest?

The General Medical Council has 40 pages of advice on professional practice for its members. Doctors have lengthy briefing papers on issues ranging from confidentiality to consent. The National Union of Journalists, the nearest thing British reporters have to a professional body, has a twelve-point code of conduct – that's only two more than Moses managed in the Old Testament.

Well, journalists aren't really professionals. You don't need a licence to practise journalism.

Individual publications and broadcasters have their own rules. The *Guardian* has a readers' editor who is allowed to investigate complaints independent of the paper's management.

The BBC has a complaints unit and over 200 pages of

editorial guidelines. They drill down into issues like deception:

> ... where there is a clear public interest and when dealing with serious illegal or anti-social behaviour it may occasionally be acceptable for us not to reveal the full purpose of the programme to a contributor. The deception should be the minimum necessary in proportion to the subject matter.

So that's crystal clear. The problem is not so much that every moral issue in journalism is contested – like what's in the public interest – it's more that moral issues barely get raised at all.

Take Clive Goodman, the former royal editor of the *News of the World*. His inside knowledge of palace affairs was the envy of colleagues, until he went to jail for intercepting mobile phone calls. Those calls had uncovered, among other more compelling revelations, the fact that Prince William had injured a tendon in his knee.

In fact, it was Goodman's over-confidence to bury this utterly futile piece of information in the diary column of his newspaper that first alerted the Prince and his staff to the possibility that someone might actually be engaging in a spot of electronic eavesdropping. A week or so later Goodman was finally caught out when he ran a story that another reporter, ITV's Tom Bradby, realised could only have come from someone listening in on his voicemail to the Prince's mobile phone.

Before you think there's no honour among thieves, there is! Bradby is as decent and honest a man as you could meet within or without journalism. Goodman simply broke the law.

Journalists, of course, are hardly alone in their snooping. Corporate espionage is big business. The care with which large corporations conduct their own security arrangements makes one wonder if such techniques are not unknown in many more areas of business than journalism. Because the information they acquire tends to end up in the public domain, journalists are just more likely to be found out.

▮ Who are these people? ▮

Most people asked to name a media mogul would reply simply, Rupert Murdoch. In Britain, Murdoch's News Corporation has about a third of the newspaper market. He owns *The Times* and its Sunday equivalent, as well as the *Sun* and its Sunday equivalent, the *News of the World*.

Murdoch is an Oxford-educated Australian who now has US citizenship and whose collection of world media goodies includes teen internet destination MySpace, publisher HarperCollins and global financial information provider Dow Jones, publishers of the *Wall Street Journal*.

His Fox network's most famous product is *The Simpsons* and as C. Montgomery Burns notes ruefully during one episode: 'I guess it's impossible for one man to control all the media. Unless, of course, you're Rupert Murdoch.'

Murdoch's company is a global corporation. Its senior executives move countries, launch new products, revive ailing parts of the empire or shut them down in exactly the same way as senior executives in any multinational. And editors are simply executives. They could be producing baked beans. In Britain, its market strength is at a point where it begins to draw accusations of monopoly power. It's unlikely Murdoch would be allowed to own another British newspaper.

A News Corp. subsidiary, News International, owns nearly 40 per cent of BSkyB, run until 2007 by Rupert's son James. Sky turns over £4 billion a year and airs Britain's original rolling news channel, Sky News. Sky News gets less than 0.05 per cent of audience share. Ironically, Sky is one of the biggest newspaper advertisers around, spending a few million a year trying to entice new subscribers.

A fifth of the newspaper market is owned by Trinity Mirror, which has the *Mirror* titles, the *People*, the *Daily Record* and the *Sunday Mail*, as well as a slew of local papers.

Another fifth is controlled by DMGT, chaired by billionaire Jonathan Harmsworth, fourth Viscount Rothermere, and great grandson of the man who helped start both the *Daily Mail* and the *Daily Mirror*. DMGT's subsidiary Associated publishes the *Daily Mail*, *Mail on Sunday* and London's *Evening Standard*.

That's a little less than three-quarters of Britain's national newspapers in the hands of three corporate owners.

When it comes to television, it's a bit more democratic. The public are in charge – at least nominally. The taxpayer-funded BBC is the dominant player. Channel 4 is funded by advertising, but is owned by the state.

ITV is a plc, formed from a bloody and bitter merger of local television companies. And Channel Five is majority-owned by Germany's RTL, which has TV stations across Europe. These are what are known as public service broadcasters, obliged to provide a mixed diet of news, current affairs, arts and other programming around the entertainment shows on which they rely for audiences. Public service is the toll the government exacts for giving them access to the airwaves – a justification that disappears when TV goes digital in the UK in 2012. Still, at the end of 2006 about half Britain's 60 million TV sets were good old-fashioned non-digital tellies getting just five channels.

The BBC makes the majority of its own programmes but is obliged to buy some in – though not the news. ITV has its own production company but buys in programming and Channel 4 buys all its programmes. Both channels get their news from ITN, which is basically a production company that specialises in making news programmes. ITN is owned by ITV and three other media companies. Confused?

Well, try this. In 2006, Sky bought nearly 18 per cent of ITV's shares. Might they be willing to swap those shares with RTL for a controlling stake in Channel Five? These are the kinds of games CEOs and their finance directors play in their private jets.

In the world of digital TV, there's Sky with 8 million subscribers and rising, and Freeview (yes, Sky owns a small chunk of that too, along with the BBC and others) which just sells set-top boxes.

But as far as TV goes, all you really need to know is that news is an add-on – about as popular as newsreels were with Hollywood studios and cinema audiences. ITV spends about £30 million a year on national and international news out of a programming budget of nearly £1 billion. Ironically, the only people who don't have to produce any news – but do anyway – are Sky, and they spend rather more.

▌▌ How profitable is the media? ▐▐

Before you take your pension and throw it into media stocks, are the people who own the media getting rich off it, or is the media just owned by rich people?

Keith Rupert Murdoch got his first break in life by being left a small South Australian newspaper by his journo dad – Sir Keith – the *News*. It wasn't exactly a rags to riches story, in that being left a real newspaper is still a better legacy than being left, say, a rolled up copy of a newspaper. From that modestly affluent beginning, Murdoch went on to carve out an Australian newspaper empire in the 1960s. Then at the end of the decade, he bought the *News of the World* and then, to get his presses rolling seven days a week, the *Sun*.

Turning the *Sun* into a tabloid version of the *News of the*

World made it an overnight success. The *Sun* gave him the cash to go into the US in the 1970s and it has carried on funding his empire ever since. Not everything he touched turned to gold, but when it didn't, he got rid of it.

At the start of the 1990s, he came close to going under. Starting satellite TV in the 1980s, battling the print unions at Wapping and kicking off the Fox network nearly bankrupted News Corp. One 1991 biography of him was titled *Murdoch: The Decline of an Empire*. A year later it was reissued as *Murdoch: The Great Escape*.

Here's how Murdoch himself described to a *Financial Times* reporter the deal-by-deal journey to a global media empire:

> We start with the written word. Then we get to TV, originally with the idea that it will protect the advertising base and it then progresses into a medium of its own with news, programmes and ideas. You then look at TV and you say: 'Look, we don't want to just buy programmes from a Hollywood studio, we'd better have one.' Then comes the issue of people who are going to deliver your programmes. Cable is consolidating ... Instead of having twenty gatekeepers, you are going to have three or four. For content providers, that is very bad news. So, you try to protect yourself in having some distribution power.

Murdoch personally owns nearly 15 per cent of News Corp. stock, but he has gerrymandered the company's voting system to give his family 60 per cent of the vote. The simple truth is that he does make money out of the media, a lot of it, but some parts of his empire are more profitable than others. *The Times* haemorrhaged cash for years. The *New York Post* loses money. When he owned it first time round, from 1977 to 1988, Murdoch doubled the circulation but lost $150 million by his own reckoning. New York advertisers just didn't like the readers he was bringing in.

Today the *Wall Street Journal* is barely profitable. But Mr Murdoch didn't get rich owning loss-making media businesses. Sky generates handsome profits, as do his tabloids. He's managed to expand without ever losing control to fund managers and investors in search of quarterly reports.

For two-thirds of Britain's biggest media owners, starting out owning a newspaper definitely helps. Lord Rothermere began with a bunch of them when he inherited the family business from his father. In 2007, Rothermere owned getting on for 60 per cent of DMGT. Lord Rothermere's media wealth may have been passed down the generations, but although DMGT continues to generate revenues and profits, it's staring at the same problems all media companies face today.

Its traditional national newspaper business is losing ad revenue amid declining readership (although it's outperforming rivals), the same problem is hitting its regional newspapers and its online businesses aren't generating enough cash to make up the shortfall. Still, while DMGT makes money, Lord Rothermere's media moguldom is just an accident of birth.

Odd one out, and the most troubled, is Trinity Mirror – a media corporation that isn't owned by someone whose dad was in the newspaper business. It's run in the interests of shareholders and in the current climate that means cutting costs, selling old assets (like local newspapers) and investing in new ones, like websites.

Strangely enough, cost-cutting is pretty much the strategy over in TV land where ITV still makes money, but less and less of it. They struggle with a bit more regulation because if you want to advertise on British telly on any scale, you pretty much have to go to the single biggest commercial channel, ITV, despite its declining audiences, because the BBC doesn't take ads.

At Five, owners RTL wonder why it can't make money the way the corporation's other European assets do.

In all of this, newspapers and TV stations, websites and radio are bought and sold, change hands or get shut down. For the consultants and bankers who advise on these deals they are just platforms for making money, either from people with something to sell (advertisers) or from the audience itself (subscribers). These are revenue models and you can mix them in whatever proportions work. You can own the platform or what appears on it, or both.

Some people are looking to outsource costs, others to buy duff companies, freshen them up and sell them on. But the old ways of making money from the media are under pressure, and owners – even the man who memorably introduced himself on *The Simpsons* as 'billionaire tyrant' Rupert Murdoch – aren't exactly sure what the new ways are and how much profit they will generate.

Many aren't looking for money, but something else entirely. Power.

CHAPTER SIX

The Myth of Media Power

[Press power] is a flaming sword which will cut through any political armour ... That is not to say that any great newspaper or group of newspapers can enforce policies or make or unmake governments at will, just because it is a great newspaper. Many such newspapers are harmless because they do not know how to strike or when to strike. They are in themselves unloaded guns. But teach the man behind them how to load and what to shoot at, and they become deadly.

Lord Beaverbrook

The old canon of respectable journalism is that reporters are entitled to their own opinions but not to their own facts. But journalism is always playing, and often losing, a complex game of brinksmanship between respectability and readers.

Editors may want professional esteem, but their proprietors want something else: power – the power to make or break governments, the power to have their opinions heard, the power to set the public affairs agenda.

There is little doubt that Rupert Murdoch has more influence over public debate in Britain and the US than, for instance, you or I. The question is, to what extent does the press control that agenda? How does ownership of the media confer power, and exactly how powerful are the media moguls? And does the relationship between media ownership and power make our media inherently untrustworthy?

The answers, perhaps surprisingly, aren't as simple as you think. Media power is indeed a significant social force, but, as Beaverbrook implies in the speech quoted above, it is only as effective as the person behind it. And in democracies, the media doesn't vote governments out – that is the prerogative of the electorate.

Media power is brought to bear on politics in two ways. The first is to frighten or bully politicians. The second is to influence and shape public opinion.

The politician most frequently accused of pandering to the media, or more particularly to the owner of News Corporation, Rupert Murdoch, was Tony Blair. Fittingly, perhaps, Blair devoted the last major speech of his decade-long term of office not to his other favoured topics of foreign policy, or climate change, or Africa, but to the media.

I was in the small audience as Blair confessed that he had curried favour with newspaper editors and proprietors – particularly Rupert Murdoch:

> We paid inordinate attention in the early days of New Labour to courting, assuaging and persuading the media. In our own defence, after eighteen years of Opposition and the, at times, ferocious hostility of parts of the media, it was hard to see any alternative ...
>
> I am going to say something that few people in public life will say, but most know is absolutely true: a vast aspect of our jobs today – outside of the really major decisions, as big as anything else – is coping with the media, its sheer scale, weight and constant hyperactivity. At points, it literally overwhelms ... People don't speak about it because, in the main, they are afraid to.

Blair argued that the media has changed radically in the last decade, so much so that media management is now a much more significant and challenging job for a government than it was when he first arrived at Number 10:

You have to respond to stories also in real time. Frequently the problem is as much assembling the facts as giving them. Make a mistake and you quickly transfer from drama into crisis.

In the 1960s, believe it or not, the government would sometimes, if there was a serious issue, have a Cabinet meeting that would last over two days. It would be laughable to think you could do that now without the heavens falling in before lunch on the first day.

Things also harden within minutes. I mean you can't let speculation stay out there for longer than an instant.

He went on to call for some form of regulation that would hold the media to account for its accuracy, its balance and the quality of its reporting.

The reaction to Blair's speech in the media was instant and dismissive. The kindest assessment was probably delivered by the *Guardian*: 'Right sermon, wrong preacher.' Stephen Glover in the *Daily Mail* delivered the unkindest:

One cannot help admiring the sheer magnificent self-delusion that runs through his argument ... defended to the last by his old friend Rupert Murdoch, he yet tries to represent himself as a victim, and to pin the blame on the media for his own mistakes. Even in his final days the old rogue has not forgotten how to spin the truth.

It was the kind of speech, criticising sensationalism and inaccuracy, which could have been given at almost any point in the history of the media. Blair even acknowledged that himself:

This relationship has always been fraught. From Stanley Baldwin's statement about 'power without responsibility being the prerogative of the harlot throughout the ages', back to the often extraordinary brutal treatment, if you have ever read it, meted out to Gladstone and Disraeli, through to Harold Wilson's complaints of the sixties. The relations between politics and the media are – and are by necessity – difficult. It is as it should be.

You can accuse Blair of courting the media too much, but you can hardly blame the guy. Just look at the recent history of British general elections.

▮ Light bulb man ▮

The British general election campaign of spring 1992 was one of the tightest in living memory. Margaret Thatcher had been dumped by the Conservative Party and replaced by John Major. The economy was dipping. Neil Kinnock had modernised the Labour Party after a decade out of power.

Polls put Labour a couple of points ahead. In the course of the campaign, 50 polls were conducted by six different companies for a variety of news organisations – and more than 40 of them put Labour ahead of the Conservatives. A couple of days before the election, the polls still put Labour's lead at 1 per cent.

The Conservative daily press (the *Daily Star*, *Sun*, *Daily Mail*, *Daily Express*, *Daily Telegraph* and *The Times*) had rallied to the government and fought Labour bitterly throughout the campaign. The *Sun*, the single most popular paper in Britain, sold 3.5 million copies a day.

Questions of 'framing' or 'unconscious bias' didn't really come into it. When Michael Foot was leading Labour in 1983, the *Sun* had asked, 'Do you really want this old fool to run Britain?' And in 1987, it had reported, 'Why I'm Backing Kinnock, by Stalin'. This time it chose the day before the election to report that a psychic had contacted Karl Marx, Chairman Mao and Lenin to confirm that they were all lining up behind Labour from beyond the grave.

It wasn't just the *Sun*. That same day, the *Daily Express* ran a headline, 'Let Bogus Migrants Stay', quoting a small

London-based Turkish language newspaper saying that one Labour MP had told it that she would press for a general amnesty for illegal immigrants.

On polling day itself the *Sun* ran a famous front page with Labour leader Neil Kinnock superimposed on a light bulb, saying, 'If Kinnock wins today will the last person to leave Britain please turn out the lights'. Nine pages were devoted to a 'Nightmare on Labour Street'. A box at the top said the election was a 'photo-finish'.

But the *Sun* was wrong. When all the votes were counted, it was the pollsters who came away blushing. The Conservative share of the vote was nearly 8 per cent more than Labour's. The polls had misjudged the gap between the two main parties by nearly 9 per cent.

This polling discrepancy did not stop the *Sun* from revelling in its victory. That weekend it ran a headline claiming it was the *Sun* 'wot won it!' The story modestly reported: 'Triumphant MPs were queuing yesterday to say "Thank You My Sun" for helping John Major back into Number 10.'

It wasn't just the *Sun* that was convinced that this was a media victory. A *Sunday Times* columnist observed: '... there is serious evidence for the first time in election history that the Tory tabloids may indeed, as Labour leaders are already complaining, have influenced how the nation voted.'

The Conservatives' former treasurer, Lord McAlpine, penned a column declaring the 'heroes' of the campaign to be Kelvin MacKenzie, editor of the *Sun*, Sir David English, editor of the *Daily Mail*, Sir Nicholas Lloyd, editor of the *Daily Express* 'and the other editors of the grander Tory press'. McAlpine continued:

> Never has their attack on the Labour party been so comprehensive ... This was how the election was won and if the politicians, elated in their hour of victory, are tempted to believe otherwise, they are in real trouble next time.

The column was quoted in Neil Kinnock's resignation speech, when the Labour leader said that 'the Conservative-supporting press has enabled the Tory Party to win yet again'.

An election that the pollsters had suggested was on a knife-edge had actually been a cakewalk for the Conservatives. But the myth arose that it had been a close contest, won by the power of the press. Dave Hill, the Labour Party's PR man, went so far as threatening complaints to the newspaper regulator, the Press Complaints Commission.

Of course, besides the campaign it could be argued that a media dominated by a pro-Conservative partisan press had moulded people's views. But were people really so malleable? And was the media really so powerful?

Academic John Curtice's compelling analysis of the 1997 general election concluded that the press did make a very small difference to voters' choices, not so much during the campaign but in the longer term. He reckoned:

> Even if there is an imbalance in the proportion of persons reading pro-Labour or pro-Conservative newspapers, the net effect on the balance of party popularity over any period of time tends to be small if evident at all. Above all, we have seen that a pro-Labour imbalance in the press in the 1997 election was insufficient to avoid a decline in Labour's overall level of electoral support. And it is wholly unable to explain why there was a rise in the Liberal Democrats' [Britain's third party] support at all.

Yet politicians – and, naturally, journalists – seem unable to dismiss the approval or disapproval of the media as a defining factor for the public. *Guardian* political columnist, Polly Toynbee, spoke for many when she painted this typical picture of media power:

Historians underestimate the degree to which the strange nature of the British press has warped the course of events of the last Tory century. Beaverbrook's brute power and Northcliffe's promise to give his *Daily Mail* readers 'a daily hate' set the tone for a politically distorted press, bent against every Labour government. They brought down Attlee, reduced Harold Wilson to extreme paranoia and kept Kinnock out. John Major names the day of his downfall from the moment Murdoch turned against him and chose to give Blair a chance.

Is the press really that powerful?

▌ The spin doctors ▐

> You cannot hope
> to bribe or twist,
> thank God! the
> British journalist.
> But, seeing what
> the man will do
> unbribed, there's
> no occasion to.
> *Humbert Wolfe*

The media is getting the lion's share of the blame here for being lying, cheating middlemen. But that's giving them too much credit. Journalists operate within real and imagined time constraints. They are asked only to fill space or time, to interpret the goings on in the world around them in a way that will attract an audience.

Often, more often than you might expect, the realities they choose to pass on or dress up are the ones that are most understandable to them and therefore likely to be most understandable to their audience. And these are likely to be the ones that have been packaged and delivered to them in the most intelligent form. When I say 'intelligent', here, what I mean is 'simple'. The way to get a journalist to understand a story is to make an often-complex reality sound simple.

This is how it works. Imagine Jim, our young, enthusiastic reporter at a trade magazine covering, say, the farming industry, sitting at his desk. His phone rings:

'Hello, Jim Hack …'

'Hi, Jim,' tinkles a west London Bridget Jones accent on the end of the line, 'Jemima at Target, Treacle and Dumpling, and I'm just calling to see if you received the release I emailed you yesterday afternoon.'

Jim, bored and busy: 'Ah, yes. No … maybe. What was that?'

'It was just about AgriChem's new tomato fertiliser. Its non-genetically determined absorption osmosis techniques are revolutionising the cherry tomato germination cycle by compressing conventional osmotic standards …' Jemima says breathlessly, hoping to get to the end of her spiel, already pitched four times this morning, before Jim hangs up on her.

'Sorry …' says Jim, distracted by a Facebook invite giving details of a colleague's leaving drinks.

'Well, AgriChem did an independent study with 160 farmers, and it showed that cherry tomato farmers are going to see huge profit increases over the next year as they see yields on glasshouse crops skyrocket …'

Jim's ears prick up as the keywords profit, yields and skyrocket ring alarm bells in his brain. 'A study?' he says, 'What does your press release look like? Could you email me another copy?'

Jemima is on a roll. 'The study is being launched this afternoon. I'm wondering if you might be free for half an hour to meet with AgriChem's CEO. He'd love to show you how it works and we have a number of farmers coming along who'll be happy to talk you through how this new fertiliser will revolutionise their businesses. It's half two in Charlotte Street.'

Jim calculates: half two in Charlotte Street means a glass of something with the fertiliser story. File by five. Leaving drinks by half five.

Hey presto, AgriChem's revolutionary non-genetic osmosis accelerator gets 540 words in next week's edition.

That is how it works, more or less, at every level, from the trades to the glossies. The majority – some studies estimate as much as two-thirds – of the stuff we read in our newspapers or magazines, hear on the radio or listen to on tonight's TV news, began life as a media release. Planted in a lazy and compliant media only too willing to run with the line seeded by an army of professionals whose sole measure of success is the number of column inches about their client that appear in the press.

Not every story is as simple to sell or as easy to target as a fertiliser sell to a trade hack, though.

If you want to sell a new government to the country, it takes a little more luck and gumption, but it can be done. Just ask Alastair Campbell.

According to Campbell's diaries, a subtle word in the ear of the journo in chief, Rupert Murdoch, can do wonders. Prior to the election that brought Blair to power in a landslide, Campbell travelled with him across the globe to the exclusive resort of Hamilton Island in Australia, to meet and greet the mogul and his top cronies. This is what Campbell had to say about the meeting:

> JULY 1995: I got a fascinating glimpse of the way editors work around him [Rupert Murdoch]. I said to Murdoch that it was an important speech, that TB [Tony Blair] had put more of himself into it than any speech outside party conference and I reckoned it would go big ...

A couple of minutes later, RM spoke across a few people to Stuart Higgins [*Sun* editor] and later to Peter Stothard [*Times* editor], and said it was a big speech TB was delivering tomorrow. Of course, because of the time difference they would be getting it out of London and putting it straight into the paper.

Both editors disappeared for a couple of minutes and told me proudly they had ordered London to give it a good show ... I was pleased, but the truth was they had been spun by their boss who had been spun by me.

Was the diary claim just Campbell's hubris? Well, *The Times* headlined the appearance, '"Radical" Blair Lays Claim to the Thatcher Inheritance' and carried a 2,000-word extract from the speech.

In 2006, a former Downing Street press officer wrote that during Tony Blair's premiership, Rupert Murdoch 'seemed like the 24th member of the cabinet'. Admittedly the press officer had never met Murdoch, but that didn't stop him declaring:

> ... all discussions – and let us hope the word 'negotiations' isn't more appropriate – with Rupert Murdoch and with Irwin Stelzer, his representative on earth, were handled at the very highest level. For the rest of us, the continued support of the News International titles was supposed to be self-evident proof of the value of this special relationship.

But column inches in the *Sun* or *The Times*, as we know from studies like John Curtice's, carried negligible weight with voters. So if Murdoch's media holdings couldn't convert people, what was he worth to a Labour prime minister?

Undoubtedly, underlying Labour's preoccupation with the importance of the owner of the *Sun* and *The Times* was the looming shadow of the 1992 defeat. But Murdoch, unlike the owners of the *Daily Telegraph* or the *Daily Mail*, had shown himself to be willing to switch sides. He was also – unusually for a businessman – interested in politics and policy.

Murdoch was actually a touchstone against which the impact of decisions could be quickly measured. Tony Blair granted him something of the power that Walter Bagehot ascribed to a constitutional monarch – 'the right to be consulted, the right to advise, and the right to warn'.

Yet at the end of his premiership, as we've seen, Blair saw fit to quote Stanley Baldwin, who accused the press barons of his time, Lords Rothermere and Beaverbrook, of enjoying 'power without responsibility'. Baldwin's 'harlot' speech had been delivered more than three-quarters of a century earlier in a hall beside Broadcasting House and it marked a Blair-like moment for three-time Prime Minister Baldwin, and the summit of the 1930s battle for political power waged by one of the most formidable press barons of the 20th century, Lord Beaverbrook. That story itself tells us a lot about the real nature of media power.

■ Flaming swords, political armour, etc. ■

The quote that began this chapter, from Max Aitken, Lord Beaverbrook, was talking about press power. The possessor of the loaded gun was not Aitken himself but Harold Harmsworth, a barrister's son, who had risen to become the first Lord Rothermere – creator with his brother, Alfred (who was bumped into the aristocracy as Lord Northcliffe), of two national morning papers, the *Daily Mail* and the *Daily Mirror*.

At the beginning of the 20th century, the Harmsworth brothers had mobilised popular opinion in press campaigns against food taxes, against the House of Lords, and, after the First World War, against government spending. Not only had the two brothers got peerages, Harold had served as Lloyd George's air minister. By 1930, Rothermere's media empire included the *Daily Mirror*, the *Daily Mail* and the *Evening News*. He could also call on the *Sunday Pictorial* and the *Sunday Dispatch*. He was reputedly the third wealthiest man in Britain.

Rothermere and Beaverbrook had a mutual admiration for each other, but their alliance was a complicated affair. Rothermere had a joint financial interest in the *Daily Mail*'s chief rival, Beaverbrook's *Daily Express*, and saw him as not simply a collaborator or competitor, but something of a protégé.

Beaverbrook, Canadian by birth, sought to surpass his old master's achievements in newspapers with the *Daily Express* (which he did) and in politics by using press power to reach the summit of Imperial British power – the premiership (which he didn't).

During the First World War, he was brought into Lloyd George's administration as Minister of Information with cabinet rank, having demonstrated something of a talent for propaganda. But the experience also taught him a lesson: 'The only prize worth anything is the Premiership. A man in any other post is only wearing the Prime Minister's livery.'

Beaverbrook's aim was to replace Conservative Party and opposition leader Stanley Baldwin, 'a rich man without ideas who has been twice Prime Minister', according to a contemporary and neutral commentator.

His campaign was called the Empire Crusade and to take it further in 1930 he announced the creation of the United Empire Party and adopted the red Crusader symbol on the masthead of the *Express* that remains there today. In early January 1930, one of Rothermere's Sunday papers claimed that there was 'no man living in this country today with more likelihood of succeeding to the Premiership of Great Britain than Lord Beaverbrook'. Returning the favour, Beaverbrook called Rothermere 'the greatest trustee of public opinion we have seen in the history of journalism'.

The United Empire Party's opening manifesto went out

to 6 million British homes, not as propaganda but in the news columns of the 'Beavermere' press. It was topped by banner headlines, buttressed by editorials and addressed not only to men but also to recently enfranchised women voters. It planned to contest half the seats in the country.

In making his appeal for contributions to the new party, Beaverbrook made the radical declaration that all receipts and expenditures would be publicly audited, and challenged other parties to be equally frank about their finances.

Within a day, contributions totalling tens of thousands of pounds had been raised – unsurprisingly, since Beaverbrook had taken the precaution of already ensuring pledges of nearly £40,000. The Beavermere papers claimed that five Conservative members of Parliament had switched allegiance to the United Empire Party.

The two press barons' crusade against Stanley Baldwin culminated in a political showdown in the safest Conservative seat in the country – St George's, Westminster. Buckingham Palace fell within the constituency boundaries and it was considered so safe that no Labour or Liberal candidate bothered to stand.

Although there was an official Conservative candidate, industrialist Sir Ernest Petter put his name on the ballot as an independent to register a modest protest. No one might have paid much attention to the election, but then, as *Time* magazine reported:

> With a single blow of his hard Canadian fist, Baron Beaverbrook shattered the idyllic calm ... Sir Ernest was told [by Beaverbrook] that he could either get up on his feet and fight the press lords' battle against Stanley Baldwin or they would smash his candidacy by putting up a third Conservative candidate. What could he do but accept the aid of two such very rich men?

Petter now found himself the pawn in a bigger political battle. On 28 February 1931, Beaverbrook's *Daily Express* announced that Sir Ernest would run 'in opposition to Mr Baldwin's leadership and policy'. Rothermere's *Daily Mail* added: 'His object is to make the Conservative Party leadership the issue of the by-election on account of Mr Baldwin's lack of power and ability to lead the country out of its present difficulties.' St George's was to be the field of battle between the media and the politicians.

Faced with an election campaign against overwhelming press opposition, the official Conservative candidate folded and dropped out. Baldwin faced the prospect of Sir Ernest being handed victory without a fight, a victory that would destroy his leadership.

Baldwin's nerve almost failed him and he told a colleague he was going to resign, but finally a candidate did come forward from an unexpected quarter. Alfred Duff Cooper knew Beaverbrook (he was godfather to Duff Cooper's son). His wife had been admired and employed by the press baron. Beaverbrook – 'in the friendliest manner' – tried to persuade him not to stand.

But once Duff Cooper entered the ring, the gloves came off. As Duff Cooper later wrote of the *Daily Express*, *Daily Mail*, *Evening Standard* and *Evening News*: 'These four papers were my chief opponents, and every issue of them was devoted to damaging my cause.'

Just to show how well they did it, the *Express* reported the beginning of his campaign under the headline: 'Mr Duff Cooper's 44 Listeners: A Meeting Fizzles out at St George's.'

Now he found himself running against the press barons, Baldwin fought on the issue of press dictatorship.

The *Express* put its response in a leader column:

Q. The *Daily Express* and the *Daily Mail* are trying to persuade Mr Baldwin to retire and make way for his successor. Is that dictatorship?

A. The Baldwinites say so.

Q. But *The Times*, *Telegraph* and *Morning Post* say that Mr Baldwin should not resign. Is that dictatorship?

A. No. That is loyalty.

The attacks prompted Baldwin's most famous speech (the last line written, it was said, by his cousin Rudyard Kipling, who had once been an adviser to Beaverbrook). The venue Baldwin chose was the Queen's Hall, which, before the Blitz, stood beside the BBC's headquarters in Langham Place. And he railed against the Beavermere press:

> The newspapers attacking me are not newspapers in the ordinary sense. They are engines of propaganda for the constantly changing policies, desires, personal wishes, personal likes and personal dislikes of two men. What are their methods? Their methods are direct falsehood, misrepresentation, half-truths, the alteration of a speaker's meaning by putting sentences apart from their context, suppression and editorial criticism of speeches which are not reported in the paper ... What the proprietorship of these papers is aiming at is power, but power without responsibility, the prerogative of the harlot throughout the ages.

As if to confirm every charge, the *Express* splashed next day with 'Sir Ernest Petter's Triumph' – a write-up of their candidate's rally in a London theatre.

Baldwin's speech was carried lower down the page, under the headline, 'Mr Baldwin Denounces His Enemies'. The *Express* editor, Arthur Beverley Baxter, had gone along to report the meeting himself, with, as he put it, 'a mind unprejudiced'.

Beverley Baxter did not include the quotes above in his report of the evening, although he observed: 'the political platform allows for over-statement and Mr Baldwin knew what was expected of him.' The innuendo grew thicker: 'He [Baldwin] made one smear at Lord Rothermere, however, that simply is not done. When he had made it, he looked furtively at his audience and licked his lips.' By the end of the evening, said the *Express*, the hall was like a 'public morgue'.

Yet, just three days later, Baldwin's candidate won the seat. Beaverbrook's challenge had passed. As former Fleet Street editor Hugh Cudlipp wrote: 'The baleful influence of proprietorial journalism was diminished. The personal prestige of Beaverbrook and Rothermere as Press barons, which rarely extended beyond their mutual genuflection, plummeted: so did their power ...'

But like all good stories, this one has a number of morals. Depending on your perspective.

If you don't accept that the media wield political power, then the St George's by-election illustrates the quixotic robustness of voter choice as a check. It illustrates too the ability of politicians to stand up against media bullying. The media barons might fulminate, the headlines might scream, the bully pulpit of the editorial pages might exhort voters to exercise their rights in one way or another, but in the end, the choice is theirs and theirs alone. Elections provide a means by which press power can be controlled, just as it should be in a democracy. Despite the endorsement of the most powerful array of newspaper comment ever to be lined up against one candidate, voters ultimately proved capable of exercising independent choice.

If you are more sceptical, then you might also note that Beaverbrook had already won political power and cabinet rank a decade or so earlier. His press interests had made his private politicking infinitely more influential than his public campaigning – he had played a key role in getting Lloyd George into office during the First World War.

The Beavermere story is not so much of the close links

between political power and press power, but of the gulf dividing them. The press barons were unable to use newspapers to win actual political power. Their campaigns may have fed their own front pages, but they were ephemeral. The Empire Crusader still sits on the masthead of the *Express*, but no one remembers what it stands for, or why it is there.

You might also argue that the social forces at play influencing voters outweighed media influence. And the setback in St George's didn't prevent Beaverbrook returning to government in the Second World War as Minister for Aircraft Production.

While the Beavermere tale is perhaps an equivocatory one for those who deny the power of the press, or at least question whether it is something we really need to worry about, the other end of the spectrum is represented by more modern media political shenanigans – in Italy, that blazing example of democracy in action. Silvio Berlusconi's all-encompassing embrace of the country's media and political life is a cautionary tale for those who don't believe ownership of media assets creates equivalent responsibilities.

▮▮ All on the same page ▮▮

Every editor or director, with his autonomy, must play the same music. We must avoid disagreements amongst ourselves, one newscast against the other, one network against the other ... We must sing in chorus on the themes that interest us ... You must understand, you top editors, that we must respond to those firing against us with a concentrated attack of all our means against them. If those who attack us unjustly ... were assaulted simultaneously by all the various media of our group, the aggression would end there.

Silvio Berlusconi

When Enrico Mentana was sidelined from his job as presenter and editor of the news on one of Silvio Berlusconi's biggest TV channels, he was asked about the power of his proprietor – and Italy's prime minister. Mentana replied gnomically: 'Television supports phenomena. It doesn't create them.'

Silvio Berlusconi's interest in media came about almost by accident. In the late 1970s, he installed a private cable channel on a housing estate he'd developed some ten years earlier. It was a success and as a result Berlusconi began buying up hundreds of tiny cable companies across Italy on his way to establishing a national network that would rival the state broadcasting monopoly, RAI. It was called Mediaset.

Berlusconi has no formal position in any of his media companies. His media power derives entirely from his 63 per cent stake in his investment company Fininvest. Fininvest has the majority share in Mediaset's broadcast empire. It also owns Italy's biggest book and magazine publisher, a financial services group, internet service providers, cinemas and European football giant AC Milan.

Berlusconi undoubtedly has bucketloads of business acumen. But that's not all he's got. The man known to supporters as *Il Cavaliere* (the knight) was part of an old and none too savoury political network. In the 1980s, his political patron was a socialist, Bettino Craxi, a man whose name became synonymous with political corruption. When an Italian court declared that Berlusconi's networks should be taken off air because they were operating illegally, Craxi postponed a visit to Britain. He used his prime ministerial powers to sign emergency legislation to prevent their closure.

Then, in the early 1990s, the *Mani Pulite* ('Clean Hands') corruption investigations destroyed the credibility of Italy's political establishment. Public prosecutors traced nearly £4 million in bribes that had found their way from offshore companies into Craxi's Swiss bank accounts. Craxi fled

Italy to live in exile. The offshore companies belonged to Silvio Berlusconi.

For Berlusconi, the threat was also an opportunity. As *Mani Pulite* removed the credibility of Italy's political parties it created a vacuum.

Il Cavaliere began polling to weigh up his electoral chances. In one poll, he discovered that he had nearly total name recognition with Italian voters, while only half knew the name of the country's stopgap prime minister. Another poll, asking Italian school children to list their heroes, put Berlusconi top. Arnold Schwarzenegger and Jesus Christ came in second and third.

Berlusconi was not afraid of politics or wary of the Italian public. He'd acquired a taste for popular adulation while president of AC Milan. Berlusconi recalled an incident before he entered politics when, after one football victory, a fan shouted: 'Silvio, if you want, we'll vote for whatever party you tell us.'

And football provided more than political inspiration, it provided a model. Berlusconi named his party *Forza Italia* ('Go, Italy!') – the words that fans chant when the national team plays. Italy plays in blue, and in another nod to the national obsession, party members were the *azzurri* ('the blues').

Berlusconi traded outrageously on his success as a club owner. Debating economic policy with an opponent who happened to be a professional economist, Berlusconi asked: 'How many Intercontinental Cups have you won? Before trying to compete with me, try, at least, winning a couple of national championships!'

Berlusconi began his political career not with newspaper ads like Beaverbrook, but with a videotape. It was sent simultaneously to all the main television networks. Like Beaverbrook, he had an advantage. He owned half of the media. Two months later, in 1994, he was Italian prime minister.

But internal rivalries, coupled with Berlusconi's indictment for alleged tax fraud, led to the collapse of the government just months later. The *coup de grâce*, a notice that he was being investigated for corruption, was delivered as he chaired a European meeting on policing. Berlusconi, it appeared, was finished.

Again he came out fighting. Every court case was challenged. His empire undertook daily editorial attacks on the magistrates who were prying into the business affairs of *Il Cavaliere* and his friends.

One of Berlusconi's most high-profile allies was MP Vittorio Sgarbi. Sgarbi also hosted a show on one of Berlusconi's channels. He made it a point to go after anyone daring to investigate Silvio and his associates. Sgarbi called the lead magistrate, Antonio Di Pietro, and his team 'criminals' who were subverting democracy.

Di Pietro became the target of bribery accusations in the Berlusconi press. Milan's daily paper, *Il Giornale*, owned by Silvio's brother Paolo, led the assault. Eventually, the accusations turned out to be unfounded and *Il Giornale* ended up paying damages and printing a lengthy retraction. But while they were going on the result was to marginalise a key anti-corruption campaigner.

Di Pietro was not the only target. *Il Giornale* called Palermo's chief prosecutor a death squad leader. His crime? Convicting Berlusconi's campaign manager of collusion with the Mafia.

Berlusconi found ways to buy off or eliminate potential critics. The host of state broadcasting's most influential evening discussion show was given a column on a Berlusconi weekly. So too was state television's chief political correspondent. Two other top-rated journalists on state TV had their programmes taken off air after being publicly criticised by the Prime Minister. Columnists for non-Berlusconi newspapers like *Corriere della Sera* and *La Stampa* were also invited to take their places on the Mediaset payroll as 'consultants'.

Court cases came and went. The endless trials, convictions and appeals bored Italians. Berlusconi, promising to cut taxes, crime and illegal immigration, swept back into office in 2001.

Back as premier, Berlusconi spent his political capital achieving two things: dominance in the news media to silence critics and muzzling the judiciary, which had threatened him and his cronies. His associates and former employees were given senior roles at the state broadcaster, RAI, handing him control over two of its three channels. Installing your cronies at RAI is something of an Italian political tradition; there is even a name for it – *lottizzazione*. But with RAI and his Mediaset channels, Berlusconi had control of six out of Italy's seven main TV channels – 87 per cent of the television audience. And television is where Italians get their news.

Even Italy's ceremonial president, Carlo Azeglio Ciampi, was concerned enough to issue a public warning: 'Democracy is not healthy if there is no plurality of information, whether in the printed press or on radio and television networks.'

The most supine coverage of Berlusconi came on his smallest channel, Rete 4. Its main news programme was presented by Emilio Fede, whose canine devotion earned him the nickname 'Fido'.

Other Mediaset channels were more subtle. Before the 2001 election, Italia 1's newscasts portrayed a country swamped by criminals and illegal immigrants. Canale 5's head of news, Enrico Mentana, was finally replaced after carrying one too many stories that showed Berlusconi in a bad light.

RAI's journalists understood who was the boss. Berlusconi got half the airtime on state news programmes, his opponents only a fifth. When Berlusconi addressed an empty United Nations chamber in New York, RAI edited in pictures of a crowd listening to Kofi Annan.

Even journalists who weren't on Berlusconi's payroll could be removed. The editor of *Corriere della Sera* was another casualty of Berlusconi. *Corriere* had covered all of Berlusconi's corruption trials – the kickbacks, the slush funds, the offshore accounts. The Prime Minister had been embarrassed.

Fiat was the major shareholder in *Corriere*. In 2002, the car company nearly went bust. After Fiat's chairman, Umberto Agnelli, went to Berlusconi for a bail-out, *Corriere*'s editor decided to 'resign'.

Berlusconi used parliament to further his business interests. When he came to power in 2001, media companies were barred from raking in more than 30 per cent of their market's revenue, and television companies were barred from operating more than two national channels.

By 2003, Mediaset's three channels were taking over a third of all television advertising revenue. A court ordered it to move its smallest channel on to satellite. Berlusconi's government brought in legislation to change the limits on advertising revenue. They were raised to 20 per cent of the entire media sector – including everything from television ads to banners on websites.

The law was so embarrassingly self-serving that Italy's president refused to sign it. It was a symbolic embarrassment. After a few minor tweaks, Berlusconi's coalition passed the law again in 2004. By 2005, Mediaset was taking nearly two-thirds of Italy's television ad spend.

In the fortnight before the 2006 general election, one of his channels was fined twice for biased reporting. It was over-enthusiasm by *Il Cavaliere*'s old retainer, Emilio Fede. Having trailed in the polls, Berlusconi came back to lose the election by the slenderest of margins.

The irony of Berlusconi was that his influence with

politicians like Craxi was not bought through the nebulous influence of his media empire, but by cold, hard cash. Berlusconi ended up seeking political power to use the legislature to defend himself against the rule of law. It was a complex trade.

▮ In the end ▮

What makes Beaverbrook and Berlusconi so fascinating is their naked use of media power. By using that power publicly, they exposed it and in doing so revealed not just its strength but also its weakness.

In the 1930s, British voters remained deeply uninterested in Beaverbrook's imperial crusade, but British politicians continued to pay him court. In the 1990s, would Italian politics have been any different had Berlusconi found a charismatic stooge to front *Forza Italia*?

As Enrico Mentana noted when he was sidelined, the media supports phenomena. It was an observation that echoed something the *Observer*'s J.L. Garvin wrote decades earlier, describing the leading media figures of Beaverbrook's day:

> The most successful of them have been experts in the art of foreseeing which way the wind is likely to blow and shaping their course accordingly. Some of them ... have been so successful in this that they have been able to persuade the public that they make the wind blow. This is the highest form of journalistic art ...

CHAPTER SEVEN

A Modern History of the Media and Trust

I now have empirical evidence for why readers can't be relied on: They're two-faced, untrustworthy, duplicitous bastards.

Jack Shafer

Believe it or not, the current crisis of trust in the media is not the first. In fact, it is probably less of a standalone crisis than it is an amplification of the more or less constant wailing from the guardians of the public's morals relating to the press and its relationships to the rest of society.

To see how the current crisis is likely to play itself out, it might be helpful to look back in time to where it came from.

In 1970, for the first time in the history of the American newspaper business, the number of papers sold each day dropped below the total number of households. In case that fact didn't register, until the 1970s many Americans were taking more than one daily newspaper.

The fact did register to the industry's bright young things. Newspaper exec Robert Marbut took himself off to Harvard Business School and when he emerged, clutching a business plan, it wasn't anything to do with newspapers.

Marbut needed backing and he approached the Harte family who owned a Texas newspaper group. They turned him down. Instead, they asked him to run the family business, Harte-Hanks. It was a smart move.

In a year, he had taken the company public, had taken it beyond Texas and doubled its size. It wasn't just that Marbut brought in all the 1970s business school stuff you'd expect: cost control, budgeting and planning. Marbut's genius was to redefine what a newspaper was. It wasn't ink, pages and prose; it was 'a package of heterogeneous information designed to appeal to a number of mini-audiences, each made up of readers who share similar values'.

He was pretty clear about what a newspaper group was, too: 'We consider ourselves information providers for information consumers. This approach frees us to utilize fully the tools of the consumer product marketer, providing tailored products to meet unique informational needs.' So much for the romance of the whirring presses and the clatter of typewriters.

Under Marbut, Harte-Hanks papers became what *Forbes* magazine called 'aggressive marketing vehicles tailored for advertisers'. Like today's newspaper executives, Marbut was worried about the future and what technology would mean for his products:

> The fact that the same technology will be used by media other than daily newspapers will mean that others could enter the marketplace for meeting information needs and encroach on the franchise of an established newspaper ... new technology will make it possible for the consumer to get his needs met in a variety of ways in the future, again setting the stage for continued fragmentation of media which could lead to further encroachment of the newspaper's share of market.

And he wasn't just worried about the competition from technology. He was worried about young readers. From 1970 to 1975, the number of young adults reading newspapers had dropped from nearly 73 per cent to 61 per cent.

To do something about it, Marbut took another bold

step. He commissioned sociologist Ruth Clark to do some serious market research. Clark knew a little about newspapers thanks to a colourful past with the Communist Party. Her husband had been foreign editor of the *Daily Worker* and the Clarks had even moved to Moscow in the 1950s before returning to live in America. Ruth Clark's break had come running polls for the Kennedy campaign. At the start of the 1970s she had worked on a very influential study of youth opinion called *The Changing Values on Campus: Political and Personal Attitudes of Today's College Students*.

Clark's research on newspapers had an equally academic sounding title, *Young People and Newspapers: An Exploratory Study*. It found widespread media alienation.

Newspaper executives were shocked to learn that young people not only trusted television much more than they did newspapers, but also that their feelings of bias in newspapers had increased. 'I put more faith in news I see on television,' said one interviewee. 'Newspapers are not well-researched. They're one-sided. On television you can see the news taking place and come up with your own conclusions.'

The real problem cutting into newspaper circulations was the collapse in the evening market. Suburbanisation, with its car commutes and radio and TV when you got home, had eaten away at evening newspapers. The surveys had identified the time constraints on readers, but these were demographic and societal changes about which editors could do nothing. Trust was not the issue here.

Working side by side with Clark was Leo Bogart, of the Newspaper Advertising Bureau and onetime head of research for a cosmetics corporation. Bogart too had seen the writing on the wall:

We have seen that the downward trends in newspaper readership are marked among younger people ... It is essential for newspapers to reverse these trends if they wish to remain a mass medium a generation hence.

Bogart did a phone poll of 3,000 newspaper readers. But the sponsors of the research wanted focus groups as well – Clark's speciality. Editors found the idea of a focus group intriguing and reassuringly familiar. They mirrored vox pops, the kind of street level interview that was a reporter's stock in trade. A dozen or so people sat in a room with a one-way mirror while newspaper executives eavesdropped on their conversation. They could then come in at the end and continue the conversation. Focus groups made people's concerns easy to grasp.

Clark thought Bogart's phone poll approach was 'mechanistic and demographic'. She thought focus group findings would help bring the numbers to life. So she interviewed ten or so people in a dozen news markets – around 120 people all up.

At the end of 1978, the two researchers presented their findings at a board meeting of the American Society of Newspaper Editors (ASNE). It was a kind of showdown. Bogart's statistics confirmed the status quo. People read newspapers mainly for hard news. For the editors, Bogart's message was not one that suggested a way out of decline.

Clark's report was the exact opposite. It may have had a characteristically clunky title – *Changing Needs of Changing Readers: A Qualitative Study of the New Social Contract between Newspaper Editors and Readers* – but it was just 52 pages long and, title apart, it was delivered in language editors could understand. Clark offered solutions, telling one group of executives:

In the study we saw new values, with an emphasis on openness, instant gratification, and realization of self-needs. These values are being shared more and more throughout the country. There is no sign that there is a return to the philosophy of self-denial. People do not seem to want to deny themselves for the good of society ... People don't know who they are anymore and are trying to find out ... They want you to help them live the rich, full life.

Clark didn't need to spell it out. Advertisers wanted these things from consumers too.

Changing Needs noted that younger and occasional readers wanted papers to be 'more attentive to personal needs, more caring, more warmly human, less anonymous'. Readers 'pleaded for more positive news about their communities, more personal coverage through human interest reporting and local columnists who care and more service information to help them in their daily lives'.

Here was a recipe for winning back trust, backed up by research. The ASNE was convinced. It sent out 5,000 copies of *Changing Needs* to its members across America.

Lighter, brighter news at the expense of turgid political fare set the trend for pretty much all newspaper editors to come. This material would win back the trust of young readers. In fact, they were responding to what a few score readers in half a dozen states had told Ruth Clark.

'Winning back trust' became a rallying cry for the newspaper industry. Once you started looking for it, lack of trust was everywhere, as one local editor wrote in 1979:

What emerges, time after time, in our ... neighbourhood meetings is that too many readers apparently do not trust us. They want to know a great deal more about us before they will pledge their allegiance. 'How can I trust you', they ask, 'if I don't know who you are?' They feel our semi-anonymous staffers come and go and have no genuine interest in the community.

And Clark's findings were repeated in another focus group study of a dozen US news markets in 1979, sponsored by

America's main national newspaper industry bodies. That survey found that trust could be restored by giving people 'news they can use'.

For Bogart, the Revlon executive turned newspaper champion, newspapers had flipped the wrong way and given up their key advantage in newsgathering:

> By proclaiming the message that the public wanted fun rather than facts about the world's grim realities ... [Ruth Clark's report] legitimized the movement to turn newspapers into daily magazines with the pelletized, palatable characteristics of TV news.

▮ Four reasons for failure of trust ▮

In 1995, the cover of the *American Journalism Review* was asking despondently, 'Can the Media Win Back the Public?' A year later a million-dollar research project was launched to investigate – wait for it – trust. What had gone wrong? Hadn't the industry followed the experts' advice?

In the aftermath of Ruth Clark's original report, newspapers had played with designs, formats and subject matter. *USA Today* was launched in 1982 as a direct result of the 'news you can use' formula. The more serious papers had appointed ombudsmen to respond to readers' concerns. Whether this would help or not was an open question – the *Washington Post* had had one during the whole Janet Cooke saga from chapter one.

In the 1990s, there were four main reasons why commentators judged that the news media was haemorrhaging trust.

The most obvious reason was the one we've already heard. The product no longer suited consumers' needs. They didn't trust what they didn't use. It wasn't just the format, it was the content.

Over time, what journalists consider important hasn't always mirrored public opinion. US research has tracked the discrepancies. Consider a typical early 1990s survey by the Associated Press asking newspaper executives to rank the year's top stories.

The Times Mirror group ran a similar survey for the public the same year. The public's lead was an earthquake in southern California. American journalists put the story eighth, just above the genocide in Rwanda. The American public didn't even put Rwanda in their top twenty. And the stories that ordinary Americans rated, like a ban on assault rifles, didn't interest editors at all.

Today, websites proudly display most-emailed and most-read stories. One web-savvy observer of the BBC runs a site that shows the percentage deviation between the prominence that editors give stories online and the number of people reading those stories. It averages about 40 per cent. But with online content, the 60 per cent divergence doesn't seem to bother readers.

It isn't just that. Permanent generational waves mean that information is always becoming redundant. For years, an editor I worked with carried in his pocket the lead-in for the day his musical hero Frank Sinatra died: 'He was the uninvited guest at a million dinner parties.' It meant nothing to me. I knew Sinatra only from a few black and white movies. When he died in 1998, the line that might have worked in 1968 meant nothing.

Likewise the lengthy tabloid obsession with football player George Best. Best left Manchester United in 1974 and details of his long slide into alcoholism required constant reminders to those who had never seen him play, that this was news with which they should be concerned. Time is constantly eroding everything from cultural references to objects of concern.

The second reason for loss of trust was a loss of trust in

all things big. The split between the public and the people who produce editorial content for them can now be measured. But what about the producers themselves? In 1995, US pollsters asked the American public about press cynicism. The response? More than half of respondents though the media was cynical. And that cynicism made people distrustful.

But the polls did not distinguish cynicism from professionalism. Were journalists who appealed to popular prejudices cynical or just being responsive to events? Were editorial assessments of politicians' motives cynical, sceptical or realistic? The polls couldn't answer this more complicated question.

Trust may or may not have been the cause of declining newspaper sales, but if it was, polling was not a good way to find out about it. In their 1987 book *The Confidence Gap*, Seymour Martin Lipset and William Schneider indicated that the problem might not be with the journalists, or the press itself, but the economic model that had come to dominate it.

The pair wrote: 'Americans display an exceptional degree of hostility toward "bigness".' For example, an opinion poll that showed 7 per cent of respondents expressing no confidence in 'business' saw it shoot up to 26 per cent for 'big business'. Lipset and Schneider pointed to a growing sense of public distrust across all institutions. The media was no different; it was just tarred with the same brush.

Lipset and Schneider showed that the American public's faith in its institutions was in synch with the national mood, the country's economy and politics. If Americans felt lousy about America, there was little reason to believe they would feel good about the media. There's little reason to think that same lesson doesn't hold in most mature democracies.

The third reason is, for press cynics like me, perhaps the readiest explanation for tanking trust: sheer ignorance. All the other reasons we have discussed may be rational explanations of why some people hold strong views about the news media. But it should always be noted in analysing surveys of the press that much public opinion is based on ignorance.

A 1985 Gallup Poll, based on interviews with nearly 3,000 Americans, concluded that around two-thirds of them did not know (or were not sure) how their paper 'felt about' more than a dozen different issues. The same survey concluded that only four out of ten people could define an editorial.

The fourth reason is that we are simply measuring the wrong thing. Perhaps trust simply doesn't matter – certainly not in the real world, the world of finance and power. Perhaps trust is a liberal preoccupation for journalists and editors, and certainly not one shared by those who matter in the media world – the owners and consumers.

That is not universally true. *Guardian* editor Alan Rusbridger prizes it and relates declining trust to the decline in newspapers. Declining trust is a symptom of moral failure, a good liberal stick with which journalists can beat themselves up. But Rupert Murdoch doesn't seem too fussed by it.

The news industry's interest in credibility – the reason for this whole book – is partly based on the oft-stated belief that 'credibility sells newspapers'. That quote came from a 1987 speech by the chairman of the American Society of Newspaper Editors' special – yes, really – 'Credibility Committee'. It's echoed today by editors like Rusbridger:

> In a modern media environment trust in journalism is extremely important, and the news organisations that have it will thrive, and those who don't will be viewed with increased suspicion by readers and viewers.

Unhappily, research doesn't seem to offer much support for

that claim. The same year the ASNE were staking their commercial lives on credibility, an academic study in *Journalism Quarterly* found that 'how often a person reports reading a newspaper or watching local or network television news is not consistently related to that person's credibility ratings for newspapers or television news'. In other words, who cares what is true and what is not?

Like approval ratings, credibility ratings are peaky. They shift from issue to issue, from day to day. Often depending on who is being polled. A newspaper that prides itself on its fairness and impartiality can shatter that reputation with one ill-judged photograph, one poorly chosen headline. But it may not matter to them commercially. The *Washington Post* and the *New York Times* are still around, despite crippling credibility crunches.

◗ Meyer's Herculean research ◖

In 2004, a former newspaper executive turned academic, Philip Meyer, wrote a very influential book for media insiders, called *The Vanishing Newspaper: Saving Journalism in the Information Age*. Meyer attempts to prove a laudable point: that there is a strong correlation between newspaper quality and newspaper profits. Meyer wanted to demonstrate that the things that made newspapers good could be measured and indexed, and that the index could be used to generate value. It was a nice try.

Meyer's work is based on something called the influence model, developed by one of his old colleagues. It goes like this:

A newspaper's product is neither news nor information. We are in the influence business. We create two kinds of influence: societal influence (not for sale) and influence on the decision to buy (for sale). But they are related, because the former enhances the value of the latter.

According to Meyer, 'if the model works, an influential news-paper will have readers who trust it, and therefore it will be worth more to advertisers'.

Meyer spends a lot of time making a point made by an old newspaperman back in the 19th century:

> If the excellence of a newspaper is not always measured by its profitableness, it is generally true that, if it does not pay its owner, it is valueless to the public.

Meyer is like a restaurant critic trying to convince a fast food chain to build Michelin star establishments by tabulating crockery size, waiting staff and kitchen garnishes. Maybe things would be better with a Paris-trained pastry-chef and sure, it'd be fun to eat off individually designed porcelain plates, but as an investor, you know you couldn't afford to run one on a scale that makes sense.

It's a magnificent effort – Herculean almost – given the data he assembles. But it fails on two counts. Firstly, 'good' newspapers as defined by Meyer have gone to the wall as well as poor ones. Distribution has been one key factor in those stories. One of the examples of good content he mentions was a children's page he developed. Parents liked it. Kids liked it. It passed all the quality tests except one. Advertisers didn't want to advertise in it.

Secondly, the financial markets don't measure 'quality'. They measure money. Ruthlessly. Financial analysts have a range of ratios and measures by which they put a price on stocks. None of them include 'quality' measures. Investors don't value a restaurant by its contribution to public nutrition or the degree to which it educates the public palate – and the same holds for a newspaper. Success may be a by-product of 'quality', but it sure doesn't guarantee it.

One of the 'quality' attributes Meyer highlights is trust, which he divides still further into believability and credibility.

It would be lovely to believe that these qualities offered an insurance policy against commercial failure. Alas, good newspapers numbered among the hundreds that have gone to the wall in the past 50 years. Their credibility, in terms of their fairness, accuracy and balance, did not save them from the ravages of the market.

Let's go further back in time to look at how the press and its credibility have influenced public opinion and vice versa, to the pinnacle of the newspaper industry's power, America in the early 20th century.

▮▯ The popular press and the swarming of the crowds ▯▮

> Men who would give little credence to a tale told them by a neighbour, or even written to them by a friend, believe what the newspaper tells them merely because they see it in print.
>
> *James Bryce*

In 1909 New York's powerful newspapers came together to oppose the election of William Jay Gaynor for mayor. He was duly elected in the teeth of vicious commentary. The result prompted James Bryce, a former White House staffer, to take up his pen and write an obituary for media power called *The Waning Power of the Press*:

> Nobody cares what the newspapers say ... Though the influence of the press, through its ability to keep certain subjects always before its readers has grown with its growth in resources and patronage, its hold on popular confidence has unquestionably been loosened during the last forty or fifty years.

Still, for a medium that had for nearly half a century been losing popular confidence, newspapers in 1909 were doing remarkably well. From the 1890s, population growth, increased literacy, mass transport, and technology had all combined to produce a phenomenal upsurge in newspaper circulation across both America and Great Britain.

But the growth was fastest at the bottom end of the market, the gossip sheets and tabloid rags – much to the chagrin of the upper echelons of society among whom media scepticism is greatest. It produced some now familiar themes, not just the lament, quoted above, that confidence was on the wane.

A month after *The Waning Power of the Press* appeared, a university professor called Edward Ross launched in with another assault on the media. Its accusation was in the title, *The Suppression of Important News*.

Ross said there were three things conspiring to drag down the media. First was the influence of the market:

> The capitalist-owner means no harm, but he is not bothered by the standards that hamper the editor-owner. He follows a few simple maxims that work out well enough in selling shoes or cigars or sheet music. 'Give people what they want, not what you want.'

Second was the influence of advertisers:

> The purveyance of publicity is becoming the main concern of the newspaper, and threatens to throw quite into the shade the communication of news or opinions.

And third, the influence of owners:

> The magnate-owner may find it to his advantage not to run it as a newspaper pure and simple, but to make it – on the sly – an instrument for colouring certain kinds of news, diffusing certain misinformation, or fostering certain impressions or prejudices in its clientele.

These were the charges that Ross argued produced the single biggest problem with the modern newspaper: 'It does not give the news.'

Ross's criticisms soon found an answer from the editor of the *Wall Street Journal*, William P. Hamilton. The market was what kept newspapers honest:

> Without readers the paper has no advertising to sell ... [and] the reader is deadly quick to detect dishonesty. In other words, no newspaper can be permanently successful, even as an advertising medium, without a high percentage of honesty, both in its editorial columns and in the presentation of its news.

Even journalistic inaccuracy found a defender, in the unlikely shape of a retired Civil War general. 'It is public denials by public men of what they told the press in private,' the old general argued, that contributed 'quite as much to the impression which many share of the inaccuracy of journalistic work as its actual errors.'

If the language is a little baroque, the arguments should at least sound very contemporary. They have been repeated, restated and recycled for the past hundred or so years.

The ground was already well trod when Silas Bent, he of the stolen telegram we were introduced to in chapter four, produced what is perhaps the definitive book on newspaper journalism in the early 20th century. It was called *Ballyhoo: The Voice of the Press*, and was an insider's account of the sensationalist malpractice of earlier times. Bent was more than a little sorry to see the homogenised, mass-produced journalism that was replacing it. What Henry Ford's production lines had done for car manufacturing, agency material and syndication were doing for newspapers.

The number of papers was shrinking, even as the circulation rose. Between 1914 and 1926, Bent reckoned, nearly 600 papers closed for business – a drop of 22.5 per cent, while aggregated circulation per issue rose 35 per cent. At the turn of the 20th century, Cleveland had had three morning papers; by Bent's time it had just one. St Louis, Detroit and Minneapolis were down to one apiece. Chicago's population had doubled while its morning daily papers had dropped from seven to two. Groups, like the one owned by media baron William Randolph Hearst, were buying up newspapers across America with the aim of slashing overheads.

Bent reported that small-town editors no longer had to rely on small-town writers and cartoonists to fill their columns and pages with local colour. Group headquarters or New York syndicates could send out editorials, health advice, comic strips and agony aunts, all packaged up for a national audience. A single report from the training camp of a boxing champion could make the front page in both Miami and Milwaukee.

Magazines with national reach and massive circulations had sprung up as corporations looked to advertise their products and services to a national audience. Newspapermen like Silas Bent turned their skills to the service of these corporations as 'public relations counsellors', associating a cause or a product with whatever story or celebrity was occupying the public.

And newspapers had been joined by a new medium – radio, whose broadcasts could bring a baseball game or a hero's welcome into American homes. The effect was homogenising. Not deliberately so, but editors and executives learned quickly that success came not from presenting a panorama of the world's events but from a close-up. If a big trial or a major disaster occurred, the public bought more papers if more space was given over to it.

The lesson shaped the great media circuses of the 1920s. Even as Bent was writing, the murder trial of Ruth Snyder had court officials providing over 100 seats for reporters.

Colour and courtroom atmosphere came courtesy of three novelists-turned-reporters. Daily moralising was provided by popular religious figures, like revivalist preacher Billy Sunday. The Western Union brought a mobile telegraph switchboard to allow reporters to cable their copy across America and around the world.

The Snyder case was a textbook example of the way coverage clustered around an event and fed off it. If it doesn't sound instantly familiar, the story was the inspiration for hit Broadway show *Chicago*, which later became both a musical and a movie.

The case itself was more prosaic. Ruth and her corset salesman lover had killed her husband, Albert Snyder, with a sash weight. There was no mystery and no celebrity. The story made it on to front pages because average readers could easily identify with the principal characters. The Snyders were average people, living in an average suburb. Their lives had been shattered by adultery and murder.

Ruth Snyder and her lover were sentenced to death by electrocution. Before the switch was flicked at her execution, a news photographer with a smuggled camera strapped to his ankle got a picture of Snyder veiled and strapped into the electric chair. It was splashed across America's front pages. Silas Bent calculated that Ruth Snyder's trial got more coverage than the sinking of the *Titanic*. Flash forward 80 years to the disappearance of Madeleine McCann.

Indeed, the Chicago murder was not the first story to exemplify the popular press's ghoulish focus on the little people and the power of human interest to unite and excite vast swathes of radio listeners and newspaper readers. In 1925, Floyd Collins fell down a cave and became perhaps the first of a long list of mortal victims of the press, a list most notably capped by Princess Diana, perhaps.

Collins was in his thirties, a tourist guide in Kentucky, whose family owned a site in the Mammoth cave complex.

He was exploring underground, looking for another entrance to the system that might attract more business. One hundred and fifty feet from the entrance, a rock fall pinned his leg, trapping him. Friends found him the next day. They took him hot food and an electric lamp was run down the steep, wet, narrow passage to give him light and a little warmth.

Silas Bent's old paper in Louisville sent a 22-year-old reporter, 'Skeets' Miller, to cover the story. When Miller got to the cave, he discovered just three men at the entrance. They were sitting round a fire, wondering how soon their friend would manage to get himself out. Miller was small enough to get down the passageway to interview Collins and his story, recounted in vivid detail, was picked up across America. The suspense over Collins' rescue made for great copy and day after day, city editors led with it. A fortnight after Miller's arrival there was a city of a hundred or more tents outside the cave. Barbed wire and state troopers with bayonets kept back the crowds. Eighteen days after Miller filed his story, even the *New York Times* carried the ending of the drama on the front page:

- Find Floyd Collins Dead In Cave Trap On 18th Day

- Lifeless At Least 24 Hours

- Foot Must Be Amputated To Get Body Out

Collins' story was the inspiration for Billy Wilder's film *Ace in the Hole*, about a cynical newspaperman who discovers a man trapped by a cave collapse. The reporter manages to delay the rescue to benefit from the fame his exclusives are bringing.

One man stuck in a hole captivated the United States. When, three months later, 53 men were killed in underground explosions at the Coal Glen mine in North

Carolina, America's national media all but ignored the story – it was just another mining tragedy.

Executives and writers at news syndicates, PRs and advertisers, and radio broadcasters all understood that to capture the public's interest it was necessary to report, comment on or illustrate the main story of the day, whatever it might be.

So when a story or event came along that promised to deliver that universal popularity, it generated huge headlines, page after page of syndicated opinion, radio coverage, and pictures in the Sunday papers and the movie newsreels. As one contemporary put it, Americans, unless they were perverse individualists, 'enjoyed the sensation of vibrating to the same chord which thrilled a vast populace'.

But the Floyd Collins drama was not the biggest media circus of the 1920s. That crown went to a story that generated more column inches than the ending of the First World War: Charles Lindbergh's flight across the Atlantic.

Lindbergh's trip was courtesy of Manhattan hotelier, Raymond Orteig. In 1919, Orteig had offered $25,000 to whoever could fly non-stop between Paris and New York. Three teams had attempted the crossing. Two had crashed on take-off. A plane piloted by a couple of French Air Force aces had only just gone missing at sea.

So, a few days after the end of the Snyder trial, three aircraft had gathered on Long Island. They waited for the weather to clear in pursuit of Orteig's prize. The *Columbia*, crewed by two veteran aviators, was held up because its backer had heard that people with blue eyes didn't photograph well and wanted to switch one of the pilots. One of the *America*'s pair of pilots was a polar explorer. Then there was the *Spirit of St Louis*, which had flown across America to get to the starting line, with a 25-year-old congressman's son at the controls – Charles Lindbergh.

The weather was poor and there was no knowing which of the three would take off first. Already though, Lindbergh was a clear public favourite. He was modest, good-looking and seemed well-prepared. In contrast to his rivals, he would be making the long, dangerous journey alone. He knew how to play the part. As he said before taking off, 'When I enter the cockpit, it's like going into the death chamber. When I step out at Paris it will be like getting a pardon from the governor.'

On the evening of 19 May 1927, Lindbergh was off to see a Broadway show, but he checked on the weather before leaving and decided that there was just a chance of clear skies next morning. Abandoning a night out in New York, he headed back to the airfield to prepare instead for his flight. His luck held. Just before eight the next morning, Lindbergh executed a rather bumpy take-off and climbed for Paris, to spend the next 33 hours out of sight and out of contact. But not out of mind, because that was when the media excitement really began.

To give just one example of the public mood: at New York's Yankee Stadium, as 40,000 boxing fans waited to see a title fight, the announcer asked them to pray for Lindbergh's safe passage. The crowd stood in respectful silence.

The story transcended national boundaries. When Lindbergh landed at Le Bourget, just north of Paris, a crowd tens of thousands strong mobbed him.

Nearly half a million men, women and children lined the streets of Paris at an official reception. Banner headlines followed Lindbergh's triumphal European progress. When he flew to Brussels, he met the Belgian king and became a Chevalier of the Royal Order of Leopold.

The next day, he flew to London. Over 100,000 people turned out to meet him at Croydon Aerodrome. He made three approaches before police managed to clear the landing strip and let him touch down.

In the United States, nothing seemed to matter except Lindbergh and his story. The day *Spirit of St Louis* touched down, the *Washington Star* sold 16,000 extra copies, the *St Louis Post-Dispatch* 40,000, the *New York Evening World* over 100,000. The *Evening World* seemed restrained in declaring that Lindbergh had undertaken 'the greatest feat of a solitary man in the records of the human race'.

A writer on the *New York Herald Tribune* attempted to put a price on Lindbergh's fame, as a professional hero. Using the typical journalistic calculus, he estimated it to be exactly a million dollars:

Vaudeville	$400,000
Cinema	$200,000
Air shows	$150,000
Endorsements	$75,000
Radio	$50,000
Books	$50,000
Press articles	$50,000
Orteig prize	$25,000

On Lindbergh's return home, a single Sunday issue of a single paper devoted a hundred columns of text and pictures to him. No radio announcer or columnist questioned the White House when it spent taxpayer dollars sending a navy cruiser to France to bring home a young pilot and his aeroplane.

In Washington, he was treated to a massive public welcome, hosted by the President. Western Union had 55,000 congratulatory telegrams – they were loaded on a truck and followed him in the parade through Washington.

Lindbergh received the Congressional Medal of Honour, along with countless decorations and awards. He was offered a couple of million dollars for a world tour by air. Hollywood studios dangled three quarters of a million dollars for a movie contract. Lindbergh didn't take up their offers.

Anyone not joining in the public reverence and acclaim kept their views to themselves.

The facts of Lindbergh's trip, romance aside, were these. He was not the first, or even the second person to fly the Atlantic. He was the 104th. The first non-stop flight had been in 1919 by two British pilots, John Alcock and Arthur Brown. The British pair had crossed from Newfoundland to Ireland. Since their flight, airships and other aircraft had made the crossing. The novelty of Lindbergh's flight was his route – direct from New York to Paris, instead of leaving from Canada, and the fact that he made the journey alone.

A couple of years later, one journalist put Lindbergh's Atlantic crossing into context: 'Stripping it of its emotional connotations, one sees it simply as a daring stunt flight – the longest up to that time – by a man who did not claim to be anything but a stunt flyer.' But in 1927, the transatlantic publicity machine was primed and waiting to raise him up.

The *New York Daily News* gave away sepia photographs of Lindbergh, 'ready for framing'. His picture was displayed in hundreds of classrooms and thousands of homes. To criticise Lindbergh was to criticise America – because thanks to newspaper, radio, telegraph and telephone, Lindbergh had achieved a kind of transcendent celebrity.

Why did Lindbergh's story become a sensation? The facts alone were hardly sufficient. Instead, it was perhaps the most famous example of the network effect in information, crossing media, each iteration amplifying the last.

Although conspiracy theorists might like to believe that editorial decisions are taken in an underground bunker by the representatives of gigantic corporations, the truth is more prosaic and more random. The selection of stories depends on the professional judgement of reporters, editors and planners. They are randomly chosen. 'Skeets' Miller kicked off the Floyd Collins story, but it wasn't in Miller's power to then roam America finding similar stories to turn into national sensations.

The importance of the judgements of some of these randomly chosen individuals – exemplified by Miller at the caves – is magnified by the decision-making of those who come later in the process. Like a popular but average pop song repeatedly played, repeated telling amplified a story. Rival stories threatened or supplanted it. Predicting which tale from thousands would end up becoming a media phenomenon was inherently unpredictable. That unpredictability could not be overcome and the consequence was a procession of stories about failed rescues, suburban murders and lone fliers. None of them added up to a body of knowledge or contained within them a secret that explained their unique appeal.

The more people thought about it, the more it undermined the high idea of journalism as a provider of rational information for the intelligent citizen.

It wasn't just former newspapermen like Silas Bent who were feeling let down by newspapers. Academics too were beginning to turn their attention to the press. In 1929 a New York University professor asked his students, 'Do you feel that newspapers are guilty of "colouring the news", pandering to the interests, and not giving us "all the news that's fit to print"?' 80 per cent agreed, 17 per cent did not. Just 3 per cent were undecided.

Athough Bent and a few others before him had attempted to quantify the content of newspapers, the first major academic survey of newspaper bias did not appear until the 1930s. It was led by Susan Kingsbury. Kingsbury divided the subject matter of stories into two categories, sensationalised and socialised. She quantified and charted, mapping the editorial priorities of American newspapers. The conclusions of her survey were dispiriting:

Most of us who have believed in democracy, who have theorized about social relations or have worked hard to reform politics, have taken it tacitly for granted that the 'public' is deeply concerned about the interests at the citizenship end of the spectrum ... we have abused the press because of its failure to give the public the facts needed for intelligent citizenship ... We shall have to reconcile ourselves to recognizing that the great bulk of the newspaper reading public reacts emotionally rather than intellectually, and has not progressed much in socialization beyond the point of sympathetic thrills to sob stories and smash ups.

But not everyone agreed. One reviewer noted that the study 'throws no light on the role of the press or the nature of news', and took issue with the patronising division between the sensational and the sober:

A factory girl lets herself be transported by the tabloids to a thrilling world of love nests, Cinderella courtships and double suicides, when she could be a credit to her parents and the Democracy if she would read about the stock market and disarmament.

It was a view echoed by William Randolph Hearst, the megalomaniacal newspaper proprietor who provided the model for *Citizen Kane*:

I believe that the people's will should be obeyed. Moreover I believe that the majority decision is essentially right. Those who differ with it should study the situation themselves and find out wherein *they* are wrong.

Still, journalists at one of his papers were instructed that their readership 'does not care a hang about tax-rates, budgets ... or scores of other subjects which may appear to be important ... Let us disregard, or cover perfunctorily, subjects which are merely important, but not interesting.'

Hearst's double standards did not appeal to another luminary of American journalism, founder and editor-in-chief of *Time* magazine, Henry Luce. The same year Hearst was writing, Luce made a speech lamenting the failures of the press.

It wasn't just the rise of dictatorships from Madrid to Moscow that gave Luce cause for concern. He felt that the complexity of modern life made more demands than ever on citizens. At the end of the 1920s, sociologists Helen and Robert Lynd published a study of Muncie, Indiana – a place they called *Middletown*. Those demands, they noted, meant that 'the press becomes more and more an essential community necessity in the conduct of group affairs'. But, reported the Lynds, far from expressing interest in the lives of their neighbours, the people of Muncie were interested in syndicated New York gossip about East Coast socialites they had never heard of.

The contradictions of a community that put distraction ahead of information was not one that journalists sought to grapple with. Their cop-out was summed up in the motto of one great newspaper chain: 'Give light, and the people will find their own way.'

From the summit of *Time*, Luce saw three main problems with journalism. Firstly, there was 'no significant restraint on vulgarity, sensationalism and even incitement to criminality'. Second, market-led journalism had 'an enormous financial incentive to publish twaddle'. Lastly, it failed to inform democracy: 'Never in the long history of Western civilisation was the purely informative function of journalism more important than it is today.' Luce proposed to do something about it. As the Second World War raged, he gave a couple of hundred thousand dollars to one of America's leading academics, Robert Hutchins.

Hutchins proposed a commission of a dozen of America's

finest minds to contemplate a solution to the problems of the press. None of them were journalists. The Hutchins Commission, said its chair, 'plans to examine areas and circumstances under which the press in the United States is succeeding or failing, to discover where free expression is or is not limited, whether by governmental censorship, pressures of readers or advertisers, the unwisdom of its own proprietors or the timidity of its managers.'

The report, *A Free and Responsible Press*, was published in 1947 and was an astute, articulate and impassioned indictment of the mass media. It asserted that the press is free for the purpose of serving democracy and that a press that shirks its democratic duties will lose its freedom. The report calls on the press to improve itself in the name of morality, democracy and self-preservation.

Unsurprisingly, the press didn't receive the report particularly well. It was almost drowned out by howls of protest. Over the half-century since Hutchins, the report has shaped academic thinking about journalism, but the practice of journalism carries on untouched. A flawed success as an analysis, *A Free and Responsible Press* has proved, as a call to action, a magnificent failure.

Then, as now, the media carries on regardless, ironically because those who made most from it, like Luce, failed to understand it as well as men like Robert Marbut. And it was Marbut's stark vision of news simply as content around which advertising could be wrapped, that prevailed. As an ironic postscript, in 1997, Harte-Hanks, the chain that Marbut led, that had commissioned the report that started the whole 'trust' ball rolling, sold up its newspapers, radio and TV stations. It dumped the stories and went into direct marketing instead.

CHAPTER EIGHT

An Ancient History of Trust and the Media

People have always had trouble trusting what they have been told. In ancient Athens even Socrates, the master of debate, discovered that people didn't want their opinions and beliefs challenged or overturned by exposure to new arguments or contradictory examples. One of his students told the great philosopher that winning arguments was 'like winning chequers; it doesn't mean you are right'.

What the student meant was that people didn't trust you enough to change their minds just because of what you said. Rational argument was just a game, and victory did not necessarily bring the winner popularity and influence. For all the wonders of Greek rationalism, the Greeks themselves never turned to their philosophers to govern them. The citizenry didn't trust them. They didn't trust themselves to argue back. They didn't trust themselves to act on the outcome of the debate.

Information, rather than opinion, is easier to interpret. When the Greeks won their victory at Marathon, a messenger ran the 24 miles back to Athens with the news, collapsing and dying after the effort. Legend records his name as Pheidippides, but it does not report that there was someone there to challenge him. No bloggers to question his motives. No fact-checkers to make sure he'd double-sourced it. The message was unambiguous and objectively credible – we were victorious. It was the original eyewitness news.

It's from the civilised, urbane world of classical Greece that we get the first idea of news and the first civilisation in which reporters were held in low esteem. 'No one loves the messenger who brings bad news,' wrote Sophocles in his play, *Antigone.*

But when it came to trust, it wasn't arguments or news but technology that Socrates felt most concerned about. The technology was writing.

Ironically, we know he was suspicious of it only because his student Plato wrote it down. Socrates felt that written words, taken from the mouth of the speaker, destroyed the bond of trust. To make his point he told a story about the inventor of writing, which gives us probably the earliest example of the kind of media criticism that has echoed down not just centuries, but millennia:

> ... you give your disciples not truth, but only the semblance of truth; they will be hearers of many things and will have learned nothing; they will appear to be omniscient and will generally know nothing; they will be tiresome company, having the show of wisdom without the reality.

Sound familiar?

▌ The Good News: the Bible as mass media ▐

In 2007, CNN carried a story about a tattooed fish. The CNN production team probably didn't realise it, but the story was a direct echo back to a particular news bulletin aired over 400 years before. Back then there was no satellite, cable or IPTV and the spelling was a little idiosyncratic. The latest technology for delivering international news was the printed news pamphlet.

Here's how one of them reported the tattooed fish story: 'A Most Strange and Wonderfull Herring, taken on the 26

Day of November 1597,' ran the headline, 'Having on the one side the picture of two armed men fighting, and on the other most strange Characters, as in the picture is here expressed.'

Yes, there was even a picture – a woodcut – to go with it. So, is the history of the media nothing more than a recurring, centuries-old fisherman's tale?

Despite the enduring pulling power of all things piscatorial, the modern mass media did not begin with a tattooed fish. In fact, it doesn't even start with what we'd think of as news. It starts at Oxford University in the 14th century, right at the beginning.

'In þe bigynnyng was þe word & þe word was at god, & god was þe word.' This is the opening line of the Gospel of St John, translated into English by followers of John Wyclif. A great scholar and master of Balliol, one of Oxford's not long established colleges, Wyclif had lived through one of the greatest natural disasters to befall medieval civilisation, the Black Death of 1348, which had wiped out almost a third of England's population.

His speciality was the Bible. He lectured on it, and regarded it as the only source of true doctrine, to be open to all to interpret and consult as a source of truth and salvation.

So why is this the starting point for a history of today's media? Because if you want to understand the importance and role of the news media, you have to understand what it replaced – religion – and how that process came about.

The Gospel was spread, as modern marketers would note approvingly, by word of mouth. It was preached. Wyclif and his intellectual heirs were trying to speed that process, but they also had an agenda. In arguing that religious authority came from scripture and scripture alone, they were making a political attack on the most powerful international social and intellectual organisation of their day – the medieval

Catholic Church. Direct access to the Bible would transform an individual's relationship to God and to their fellow believers; in short, it would prompt them to radically reappraise both their own lives and the basis of temporal authority. It would inspire action.

The medieval Church occupied much of the space now taken by the nation state. It administered education and healthcare, undertook great public projects, managed large enterprises and had its own systems of taxation and justice. It saw people through life from entry to exit. Like any overstretched organisation, the Church really wanted passive acquiescence from its membership rather than participatory enthusiasm. The Bible was the small print in the contract with God that the Church reserved the right to interpret.

Wyclif and his academic friends did not approve. They thought people deserved the news direct, the good news that is – the Vulgate, a 5th-century Latin version of the Bible. Of course, when the good book was painstakingly handwritten and in a dead language, it was practically impossible to read yourself. So Wyclif and his associates got translating. If God could be made to speak English, the English might be better made to hear him. At heart, this was an argument about the role of the free flow of information in society. If that sounds a bit academic, here's a summary of arguments against translating the Bible from one of Wyclif's contemporaries:

Translation ... will bring about a world in which the laity prefers to teach than to learn, in which women talk philosophy and dare to instruct men – in which a country bumpkin will presume to teach. Translation will also deprive good priests of their prestige. If everything is translated, learning, the liturgy and all the sacraments will be abhorred; clerics and theology itself will be seen as useless by the laity; the clergy will wither; and an infinity of heresies will erupt. Even the laity will not benefit since their devotion is actually improved by their lack of understanding of the psalms and prayers they say ... Translation will mean the demise of a major part of the unity of Christendom, the Latin language ...

In other words, society will collapse.

Wyclif's thinking recognised the importance of information, the importance of dissemination and the importance of the moral and educational transformation that could be achieved through its delivery. Media content was religious. Wyclif believed that direct access to the Bible was necessary for individual salvation. He thought people deserved access to information, the news, in order to change their lives and save their souls. These were dangerous ideas and although Wyclif had powerful protectors and died an old man, his followers were brutally suppressed. Half a century after his death, Church leaders had his body exhumed and his remains scattered.

Still, the Bible translation that bore his name was popular. It had to be copied by hand, line-by-line, page-by-page – yet over 200 manuscripts have survived to this day. The technology of transmission meant his ideas went as far and as fast as manuscript and the spoken word could go, and no further.

The bar to progress was lifted by an engraver, working in the Archbishopric of Mainz in Germany. Some say Johann Gutenberg was inspired by the metal punches used in hall-marking, but whatever triggered his inventive streak, he overcame the several problems that had prevented moveable type printing. Johann Gutenberg's ingenuity was not limited to type. To get his press working also required the invention of quick-drying ink and a way to stop the press from smudging the paper. By the 1450s, German Bibles were being printed in Germany. By the 1500s, around 30,000 books had been produced.

It wasn't just the technology that was European. The

intellectual development of Wyclif's ideas had come through another continental innovation, humanism. It wasn't just translation into English that prompted questions about motivation and information. Wyclif's faith in the authority of scripture had naively ignored the problems not just of turning Hebrew and Greek into Latin and then into English, but also of the authenticity of the text itself. Tracing back the actual texts that lay behind the Bible also challenged the status quo.

At the beginning of the 16th century, Erasmus, one of the academic superstars of the time, began a fresh attempt to translate the Gospels from Greek into Latin. It was a project with big political implications.

To give you some idea of what was at stake, the medieval Church relied on acts of penance and atonement, which it had industrialised to the extent that it sold indulgences – get-out-of-jail-free cards for sinners. The rationale for this business was drawn from scripture. In the Greek version of the Gospel of St Matthew (3:2), John the Baptist proclaims μετανοειτε (μετανοια). The translation from Greek that the medieval Church relied on was by St Jerome. Jerome had translated it into Latin as *poenitentiatem agite* – 'repent' – and that had become one of the rationales underpinning the whole indulgence business. The Hebrew/Aramaic word that stands behind the Greek has a very different meaning – 'to turn back, go in a different direction'. Erasmus, at the beginning of the 1500s, translated it as *respicite*, meaning 'become wise again, come to your senses'. In his version, the Baptist is calling for a complete change of life, not for sinners to back redemption certificates. The translation struck a chord with critics of the Church.

Erasmus had once written that he wanted ploughboys to be able to recite the Gospels. His writings, and that ambition, inspired a young Oxford undergraduate only a few years his junior, William Tyndale. Tyndale summed up his reason for putting the Bible into the vernacular: 'I had perceived by experience how that it was impossible to establish the lay people in any truth, except the scriptures were plainly laid before their eyes in their mother tongue, that they might see the process, order, and meaning of the text.'

Tyndale had an advantage – a genius for language. You can get a sense of it in his brilliant, concise rendering of three commandments from Matthew (19:18): 'Break no wedlock, kill not, steal not.'

The poetry and elegance of his language did not make Tyndale's ideas any less dangerous to the establishment than Wyclif's. The Church did not take kindly to Tyndale's substitution of 'congregation' for 'church'. For his trouble, Tyndale was kidnapped while abroad and brought back to England to be garrotted. To discourage any other 'free' translations his body was burned in public. By the time of Tyndale's death in 1536 perhaps 16,000 copies of his translation had been brought into England, a country with a population of only 2.5 million.

It was the government of Henry VIII that executed Tyndale – the same government that broke with Rome and established state Protestantism. Only five years after Tyndale's execution Henry's new Church of England was looking to win popular support for its ideological *volte-face*, and to achieve that they authorised a vernacular Bible.

It cost a dozen shillings bound, a fortnight's wages for the average labourer. The Bible was an immediate success. In the first year some 20,000 copies were printed. Six of them were made available to the London public in St Paul's. They were placed on lecterns and the crowds that gathered around them were so noisy and argumentative that readings were banned during services.

Anyone able to access a Bible was free to interpret the Gospels and discuss their meaning without guidance from the clergy. It didn't take long for this freedom to be exploited sufficiently to provoke a response in the form of legislation. An Act of 1543 attempted to limit private Bible reading to those above the rank of merchant householder. Still, there was a problem. Only the wealthy possessed sufficient judgement to interpret the word of God unaided, but only popular support could give the Church strength to resist the international power of Roman Catholicism.

To restrict readership was to cut off a vital means of communicating the new faith to the widest possible audience. When Henry's daughter Elizabeth took the throne, an English Bible was dispatched to every parish. But clergy were ordered to instruct readers 'that in their reading thereof no man to reason or contend but quietly to hear the reader'. The Bible was to inspire silent reflection rather than social radicalism.

Elizabeth's successor as sovereign took this process one step further and commissioned a massive scholarly translation to underpin both the authority of his regime and the Church he headed. James I had commissioned the translation to actively manage the dominant media content of the age: God's word. His 49 experts produced a Bible that could be read silently and privately or shared aloud in common. The Bible that bore James's name was a single politically correct translation that could be authorised. Control was exercised over its production. Even as it informed it interpreted, glossing over controversies and imposing dogmas.

The final victory of the translated English Bible in its most celebrated version was brought before the public in 1611. In the preface to the King James Bible, the idea that access to religious information was important was clearly acknowledged:

> Translation it is that openeth the window, to let in the light; that breaketh the shell, that we may eat the kernel; that putteth aside the curtain, that we may look into the holy place ...

There is no doubt that ardent Protestants like John Foxe and Samuel Mather thought that the 'art of printing' had done wonders in spreading religion.

Replacing listening and speaking with silent scanning, and face-to-face contact with the printed page, had important consequences.

Printing, of course, didn't introduce silent reading, but it did turn it into a mass phenomenon. A 16th-century professor of medicine noted the competition his classes faced from a new quarter, 'silent instructors, which nowadays carry farther than do public lectures'. He meant textbooks.

Printed sermons did not kick preachers out of their pulpits and pamphlets didn't push speakers from their podiums. But they did challenge the primacy and importance of these public but personal ways of communicating. And eventually, they surpassed them.

Pitted against 'the furious itch of novelty' and the 'general thirst after news', efforts by moralising clergy and evangelical preachers to keep Sunday special proved of little avail. And the old saying 'nothing sacred' came ultimately to characterise journalism.

Monthly papers gave way to weeklies and finally to the daily paper. By the 19th century, church-goers could often learn more about local affairs by scanning columns of newsprint in silence at home than by trading gossip outside church. Communities had been defined by the church and its parishes, before that by rivers and mountains. The wide distribution of the same information created an impersonal link between people who were complete strangers. They were readers. To listen to a speech or sermon, individuals had to come together. In reading something that was written down, people were pushed apart.

The classical accounts of political behaviour had to be revised and updated to account for a world where tribunes of the plebs were no longer speaking to a packed forum, but editing and publishing newspapers and magazines.

While community solidarity and the need to actually 'be there' were being undermined, the vicarious thrill of participation in far-off events was being enhanced. As local ties were loosened, new forms of loyalty to bigger groups were being forged.

But the high-water mark of religious publication was also the point at which the news media began to gather its disseminators and adherents. And it was around London's great pre-Wren cathedral of St Paul's, the public showcase for Henry VIII's English Bible, that the modern news media emerged. Fleet Street's geographic location is no accident.

Under the Stuarts, one bishop labelled the cathedral precincts 'the general Mint of all famous lies'. The men who hung around St Paul's Walk were 'stale Knights, and Captains out of Service, men of long Rapiers, and Breeches, which after all turn Merchants here and traffic for News'.

Probably the same kind of people the playwright Fletcher had in mind when he described 'Captain Hungry, who will write you a battle in any part of Europe at an hour's notice and yet never set foot outside a tavern' – unemployed soldiers, resting between commissions in Europe's religious wars.

The scene in and around St Paul's was recalled rather more charitably by a contemporary writer who had seen its emergence in his teens:

It was the fashion of these times ... for the principal gentry, lords, courtiers and men of all professions to meet in Paul's Church by eleven and walk in the middle aisle till twelve, and after dinner from three to six, during which times some discoursed of business, others of news. ... [T]here happened little that did not first and last arrive here.

One of those unemployed soldiers that the bishop moaned about, Captain Thomas Gainsford, became the first proper editor of a news sheet. He quickly encountered the first proper trust crisis in the media, which he tackled head-on in his own op-ed (probably another first):

> Gentle Readers; for I am sure you would fain be known by that Character, how comes it then to pass, that nothing can please you? ... If we talk of novelty indeed, you make a doubt of the verity; if we only tell you what we know, you throw away the book, and break out, there is nothing in it, or else it is but a repetition of the former week's news ...

Still it was the Bible, not news, which remained the dominant point of reference in the 17th century. Even the news that men like Gainsford and his contemporaries traded was of Europe's Wars of Religion.

Religion remained the mountain from which every intellectual and social horizon was viewed. Successful authors were mostly churchmen, whose education and part-time employment gave them opportunities for writing.

Even an exception to that rule, a political philosopher like Thomas Hobbes – regarded by contemporaries as a suspect atheist – used more than 600 biblical quotations in his great treatise on the state, *Leviathan*. Its very title is taken from the Bible's monster of the deep.

The 18th century saw a massive expansion of the media. By the beginning of the 19th another political philosopher, Hegel, reckoned that reading the newspaper over breakfast had become a substitute for morning prayer – 'the former gives the same security as the latter, in that one knows where one stands'.

But let's jump forward from Hegel's morning paper to the outskirts of Paris in 1830. A revolution has just installed a constitutional monarchy and Gustave de Beaumont, an ambitious young prosecutor, is sharing a flat with a co-worker. Eager to travel, he persuades the French Interior Ministry to send him on a year-and-a-half-long fact-finding tour of America to report on their prison system.

His flatmate tags along on a trip that takes them from New York down to Alabama and up to the Indian frontier. However, while Beaumont stays focused on penal policy, his friend is fascinated by democracy, 'its inclinations, its character, its prejudices and its passions'. He writes it all up in a book that was approving in a superior sort of way, and therefore much admired by Americans.

Here is a little bit of Alexis de Tocqueville's *Democracy in America*:

> When men are no longer united among themselves by firm and lasting ties, it is impossible to obtain the co-operation of any great number of them unless you can persuade every man whose help you require that his private interest obliges him voluntarily to unite his exertions to the exertions of all the others. This can be habitually and conveniently effected only by means of *the Bible*; nothing but *the Bible* can drop the same thought into a thousand minds at the same moment.

Actually, you've probably guessed that Tocqueville wasn't talking about *the Bible*. The word he used was *newspaper*. Although he was hardly the first to make the point, his observations make it clear that a shift had taken place between the world of the Bible and the world of the newspaper.

So, in a world where the Bible was being challenged by the newspaper, was anyone interested in the idea that newspapers might take up the Bible challenge and transform people's lives? You bet.

Ready to pick up Wyclif's baton was Henry Hetherington. In his last will and testament Hetherington denied the existence of God, condemned religion as superstitious nonsense and asked to be buried in unconsecrated ground, so it's unlikely he shared Wyclif's Christian convictions. He probably shared the view of journalist turned sociologist Robert Park, who declared that 'News is a purely secular phenomenon'.

Born at the end of the 18th century, by thirteen Hetherington was apprenticed to parliamentary printer Luke Hansard. He joined in the year of the Battle of Trafalgar, but despite war with France, Hansard's workers went on strike. Although it was unlikely to have been down to Hetherington's adolescent militancy, he nonetheless found himself caught up in radical politics. By the 1820s, he had his own printing press and by the 1830s, he was running off cheap newspapers by the thousand.

In Hetherington's day, newspapers were heavily taxed because the government wanted to stop people reading them. The reason was that they were full of scurrilous attacks on the government, the Church, the monarchy and the unproductive classes as well as containing demands for unions, better working conditions and political reform. The government dragged Hetherington through the courts, fined him and imprisoned him.

His flagship publication was the *Poor Man's Guardian*, which appeared under the banner 'Knowledge is Power' where the tax stamp should have been. Just to give an idea of what that knowledge was, here's one of Hetherington's journalists:

> The only knowledge which is of any service to the working people is that which makes them more dissatisfied, and makes them worse slaves. This is the knowledge we shall give them ...

Despite the inflammatory rhetoric, this was non-violent revolution. Hetherington, like Wyclif, thought information could prompt change, but in his world, it was the news-paper that would alter lives. As a newspaper historian noted: 'education, in Hetherington's eyes, would simultane-ously make men both politically active and give them polit-ical power.'

Even though Hetherington thought people deserved the news, that it could change them for the better, there was a touch of the Piers Morgan about him. Launching the *Twopenny Dispatch*, he promised readers that it would have:

> ... all the gems and treasures, and fun and frolic and 'news and occurrences' of the week. It shall abound in Police Intelligence, in Murders, Rapes, Suicides, Burnings, Maimings, Theatricals, Races, Pugilism, and all manner of moving accidents 'by flood and field'. In short, it will be stuffed with every sort of devil-ment that will make it sell.

Everything but alleged share tipping. Unlike the former *Mirror* editor, however, Hetherington was a teetotaller who – during a cholera outbreak – refused beer and insisted on drinking only water, a decision that took him to Kensal Green, London's earliest public cemetery.

One historian of journalism called Hetherington and his radical contemporaries publicists 'who wrote to change the world'. But any belief that they were the last representatives of a golden age of informed debate can be quickly laid to rest by reading what they wrote. They were actually secular preachers of the rabble-rousing variety.

Wyclif and Hetherington are icons for the longevity of a certain kind of social criticism – that an uninformed indi-vidual is a disengaged individual. The genre remains alive and well. Noted American media theorist Herbert Gans took the title *Democracy and the News* for his scholarly attack on the failings of journalists and journalism, a broad-side that simultaneously bemoaned the power and powerlessness of the news media. A wise reviewer commented: 'could [Gans'] problem be not with news, but with [his] dreams of how news can transform us?'

Gans is the latest in a long tradition – if only people knew the truth. The idea that the public deserve the news in order for our democracy to flourish has little currency in political theory. Historically it is a radical myth. The informed citizen has replaced the honest worker has replaced the good Christian.

You can delete as applicable: the public requires information from the news media/readings from radical newspapers/a vernacular gospel. But behind both the religious and the secular myths is the simple hope that information will transform whomsoever it touches, the touching faith that if only people could bear witness to the truth they will act for the good.

CHAPTER NINE

The Importance of Public Information

The main role of news media is to filter and aggregate information, repackaging it with some entertainment value. For example, the dry and prolix prose of police reports is transformed into a thrilling story about the latest murders. As in any other market, the type of information produced and its quantity depend on supply and demand considerations.

The goal of public relations, it's often said, is to make the best possible case with the available information. Businesses need stories to go with underperforming share prices and explanations for quarterly figures, but these numbers themselves represent a benchmark. They are where the argument starts. Analysts can use them to impose their own interpretations. Rivals can read them as freely as employees.

The public information relating to corporations and businesses is tightly regulated. But within that system of regulation, there is still the need for a safety valve. When the staggering corruption at Enron was exposed, it wasn't the lawyers, bankers, accountants and PR people who blew the whistle.

When the US Securities and Exchange Commission (SEC) finally launched its inquiry into Enron back in October 2001, it would be easy to think that everyone had been fooled. In Britain, Enron's corporate generosity had embraced both Labour and Conservative politicians, and in the US, both the Clinton and Bush administrations. It was a rainbow coalition of cash. There was nothing unlawful or ideological about Enron's political spending – in the UK, for example, it was quite modest. But it wasn't money that politicians were greedy for, so much as the association with success.

Enron also bought up media commentators and business gurus. Why have due diligence when you can have unquestioning enthusiasm, intellectual laziness and critical silence?

If only journalists had got their act together earlier! But they had. Back in 1998 after the *Observer* had gone under-cover to expose some of Enron's dubious lobbying, the paper's columnist Nick Cohen wrote:

> Enron stands out as the global market leader in squaring politicians ... Enron is up to its neck in the derivatives market ... and governments made nervous by Nick Leeson [a trader whose unauthorised trading brought down Barings investment bank] could ask agitated questions. They are calmed with campaign donations when they are in power and well-paid jobs when they retire.

No one listened. The *Observer*'s business section followed Cohen's story a few weeks later with a little piece under the heading *Manager's Maxims*:

> A company can help create its own competitive environment and its own future by leading industry-wide change. This is what management theorist Gary Hamel calls 'rule breaking' to 'get to the future first'...

The by-line said Kenneth Lay, Chief Executive of Enron, but doubtlessly a public relations professional had packaged, prepared and distributed it.

So how effective is the financial press as a watchdog? Harvard Business School professor Gregory Miller measured how frequently journalists beat the SEC in reporting accounting scams.

Miller looked at the years between 1987 and 2002. The SEC confirmed about sixteen cases a year of accounting fraud. So how many of those had the media flagged up prior to the regulator getting in on the act? About five. So 30 per cent of accounting frauds were reported in the papers before the SEC took action. Still, he wasn't dismissive of that figure: 'Some people would look at that and say, "They only find 29 per cent of the frauds? Why are they missing so many?" I think when you see how hard it is to identify a fraud – I'm impressed.'

Does Miller's study make us trust the financial media? Well not so much as investigators, but certainly as an additional valve for information. Two-thirds of the cases where journalists beat the SEC were the result of reporters writing up legal action brought by shareholders or repackaging the work of Wall Street analysts.

Only a third were the result of what the Harvard professor called 'reporter-based analysis ... the use of largely non-public sources to generate original information'. Or good old-fashioned journalism, as it's also known.

Not everyone agrees with Miller. In the world of corporate news, economists Alexander Dyck and Luigi Zingales say there is a supply side problem that leads to systemic bias between journalists and their sources, where reporters get inside information in exchange for putting a positive spin on a company's news.

They say the main purpose for gathering information on publicly listed companies is to feed speculation in financial markets. The press is simply the most public branch of that newsgathering process. Speculators profit from bad news by short selling shares. That is to say they borrow a share, sell it and offer to return it at a later date, banking on the fact that when the time comes to replace it, they can buy it for less and pocket the difference. So if you understand bad news early, you sell short on the conviction that the market will come to share your understanding by the time you have to pay back your share.

When the market is bullish, selling short is very dangerous. You may be convinced that your information means that a company is in trouble but if the market disagrees, you pay the price. So in times of stock market euphoria there will be few people looking to sell short and fewer still hunting for bad news.

Except, you might think, journalists don't stand to benefit financially by circulating negative information. So why don't they step in and fill the gap?

The reason as that in bull markets growth forecasts become disproportionately important. Businesses benefit more from presenting information positively. To achieve that, they rely on being able to control reporters' access to inside information. For reporters it's a simple matter of working out what it will take to keep the information coming.

And besides, reporters can't rely on leaks or whistle-blowers to fill the gap. Politics generates constant conflicts of interest and many political players have a vested interest in sharing news, be it good or bad. In the commercial world, these conflicts are few and far between. In the majority of cases, company insiders will want to keep the share price high, so they'll only let slip good news.

What about analysts? Surely, they can be relied on to offer independent information? Most of them work for investment banks with major trading relationships at stake.

But when the market falls, this changes. Share prices become less news-sensitive, executives get fired, corporate rivalries increase – the market for information starts producing more bad news. Selling short is a less risky business and short sellers need information to be shared with the market.

And that's how it worked with Enron. Bethany McLean, the *Fortune* reporter who wrote one of the first pieces to pop Enron's balloon, was tipped off by short seller and Wall Street insider James Chanos. Chanos had started short selling Enron from November 2000, when its shares were trading at nearly $80, to December 2001, when they could be picked up for less than 80 cents.

Dyck and Zingales picked out three lessons from Enron. One, 'there was enough public information available to raise serious doubt about the credibility of Enron's earnings'. Two, the business press 'acted as cheerleader all the way to the end'. (Before McLean's article appeared, *Fortune* had just named Enron America's 'most innovative company' for the sixth year in a row.) And three, reporters who 'question the existing optimistic consensus incur constant harassment from the target company'. Bethany McLean's editor was called by former Enron boss Kenneth Lay who asked her to spike the story. She refused. Lay died while standing trial.

While journalists don't see any real benefits from reporting negative or positive information about companies, the price they pay – in terms of inside access – is real, especially when markets are soaring. As one financial columnist put it: '... in a sense, journalists are giving their readers what they want. Though, as Enron shows, that may not always be what is good for them.'

Dyck and Zingales have a suggestion for changing that equation:

> [G]reater availability of ready-to-use public information can reduce reporters' incentive to enter into *quid pro quo* relationships, maintaining greater independence of the press even during booms.

Yes, it is all about public information.

▮▮ Public information and terrorism ▮▮

In a way, the murder of the infidel, the first on British soil, fore-shadowed what happened on 7/7. But it was strange, until I saw his dead body, it hadn't clicked that we were putting ideas into people's heads that would mean the murder of innocent people.

Ed Husain

The media isn't going to provide us with ordered, audited and relevant information. There is just no way. Instead, we need to ensure that public information is available as and when people need it.

To give a very practical example, let's look in depth at one area where public information is frequently absent and where the media are often called on to make up the information gap – terrorism.

There are many clichés around the reporting of terrorism: that the media encourages terrorism, legitimises it or demonises it; that the media inflates the level of threat to scare, or refuses to take sides when society itself is imperilled. I don't want to waste time on these clichés because I regard them as a waste of journalists' time (unless they're columnists, of course).

So how do we define terrorism? Do we include attacks on Britons overseas? Or terrorist attacks undertaken by British citizens? Issues of jurisdiction are increasingly important. Security services might choose to allow the agencies of other countries to try individuals if their own legal system is not sufficiently accommodating, or may find their freedom to act constrained where conspiracies are international. The co-ordination of investigations between agencies and jurisdictions is fraught with not just legal, but political, operational and linguistic problems.

Before giving up immediately, what interests me is our ability to report on terrorism as it affects our own society –

which is to say within the controlled environment where reporters are both citizens and observers.

Let's make a distinction here between reporting and journalism. Journalism's most important role is the packaging and marketing of information – publicity you might call it, or a better word: exposure. Journalists 'sell' and 'pitch' their stories to editors. Here, for example, are its uses:

- It can provide a platform for terrorist activity: for terrorist sympathisers and apologists; but also for the police and security services, for interest groups and occasionally for terrorism victims and the public.

- Exposure can act as a safeguard on the criminal prosecution of suspected terrorists, assessing the effectiveness and competence of the police and security services.

- That exposure can also suggest remedial action (e.g. tougher legislation, increased resources, greater public vigilance or understanding).

But reporting is different. It is not the marketing of information; it is the primary task of creating information by investigation and organising it as explanation. In this chapter I want to argue that:

- We need more reporting and more records, to give us better public understanding of the issues around terrorism.

- We've missed opportunities to debate major changes.

- Reporting alone can't carry the burden of informing the public and acting as a watchdog on the security services.

▌ The non-conspiracies around David Copeland ▐

Young man. Self-confessed terrorist. 'Normal, quiet bloke.' Admits setting out to cause fear and disruption. His dad's amazed. Says he's been transformed into a bomber by extremists. Sound familiar?

Except it's not a British-born Muslim, or convert to Islam. It's David Copeland. In 1999, aged 22, Copeland set off three nail bombs across London – each one aimed at minority groups. His brief campaign of terror left three people dead, including a woman who was four months pregnant; 129 people were injured.

As the police website on the investigation, dubbed Operation Marathon, made clear:

> The arrest of Copeland was not the end of the investigation. Officers had to establish whether he was acting alone before they could be certain the bomb threat was over. A membership card for a small (and now defunct) group called the National Socialist Movement was found among Copeland's belongings. Copeland maintained throughout his detention that he acted entirely alone and never even discussed his plans with anyone else. Police could obviously not rely on his word and so they went to enormous lengths to trace and investigate everyone he had contact with – going right back to his school days.

Copeland's murderous activities were framed by right-wing extremism but he was the instrument of his own terror. He had turned his back on the British National Party (BNP) because it didn't offer a sufficient outlet for violence. The tiny National Socialist Movement, to which Copeland belonged, had collapsed after one member stabbed another to death at a house in Chelmsford in 1998.

Two men were imprisoned for their part in that murder; one of them was named in a television documentary as a paid informant for the security services. The information he had allegedly provided related to a bombing campaign involving a Danish neo-Nazi. (The security services obviously took the National Socialist Movement seriously enough to monitor it and in doing so, they had prevented another bombing campaign.)

Although there were pictures of Copeland with leading BNP figures and although the miniature National Socialist Movement counted would-be bombers and actual murderers among its ranks, the police did not uncover evidence that Copeland had been radicalised by any of the people he'd associated with, as his father had claimed.

The BNP were not outlawed because of Copeland's association with them. The reporting of his trial made his neo-Nazism quite clear and media coverage reflected the widespread revulsion at his views and his actions.

There was one big difference between Copeland and other terrorism cases. His social isolation – Copeland was a loner and the catalyst of his own crimes. There was no network effect, no cell to amplify their impact. The reporting of his case concentrated on his mental state – was he mad or bad? The jury preferred wickedness to mental illness.

The public overall gained little positive information from the reporting of the case. But they did learn a great deal about the police investigation, which silenced conspiracy theorists and answered public doubts. Copeland was caught after a phone tip-off an hour before the Admiral Duncan pub in Soho had been blown up. Could the police have prevented that bombing? It was clear from the investigation and trial that the police hadn't had time to prevent Copeland's murderous attack.

Now the Attorney General and Scotland Yard's anti-terrorism chief tell us that we need to change the rules on contempt so that we can be better informed, or better understand the nature and scale of the threat before us. Currently, courts often act to prevent the media from covering a trial if publication would prejudice other proceedings.

I would suggest that is a poor reason for changing the rules, and that the Copeland case provides a better one.

Namely, that it shows the public how threats are assessed and how they are managed. Copeland's trial demonstrated publicly what the police had done to bring him to justice – and how they had managed their investigation.

◼I The mysterious career of Kazi Rahman I◼

I want to bear that in mind when we look at another young man currently imprisoned for terrorist offences. His case was not reported while it was being tried because of a contempt of court order. He is a couple of years younger than Copeland, born in Wandsworth, south London towards the end of the 1970s. His name is Kazi Nurur Rahman, and his family were Muslims, of Bangladeshi origin. Rahman first came to public attention in the mid-1990s, when he was a student at Newham College of Further Education. He stood trial for a murder on campus.

In February 1995, Omar Bakri Mohammed had given a lecture at the Newham College. Bakri was then leader of Hizb ut-Tahrir, a radical organisation that wants an Islamic superstate, and went on to head Al Muhajiroun, an Islamist sect that was banned in Britain in 2006 for glorifying terrorism. In 1991, during the first Gulf War, he'd been detained briefly by British police for making a veiled threat against then Prime Minister John Major. A couple of hundred students came to hear Bakri speak and according to one of them, he did not disappoint: 'Bakri ... had given one of his incendiary speeches and everyone was all worked up.'

At lunchtime the following Monday, a twenty-year-old Nigerian student, Tundi Obanubi, was set upon by a group of Muslim students and stabbed to death, just outside Newham College's East Ham building. The victim's crime, one of his attackers said later, was to disrespect the Muslim religion.

Asian students killing a young African in a forgotten corner of London didn't make much national news, but a week later it did merit a report in the *Times Higher Educational Supplement*. The story began: 'Police were this week playing down reports that the fatal stabbing of a London student was racially motivated, for fear of heightening factional tension on campus.' It quoted a member of staff:

> Concerns have also been expressed about the college not coming to terms with a group of Asian fundamentalists, some of whom are students, some from outside the college. Basically they have taken over student societies and only ever want to discuss elements of Islam in an increasingly hostile type of environment.

However, the same staff member said it was unclear if this group had anything to do with the stabbing.

The Islamic element of the story then disappeared. This disappearance is important. The original report raised serious questions about religiously motivated campus violence – a murder. The authorities played it down.

In his book, *The Islamist*, Ed Husain gives a detailed account of the murder of Obanubi and its context. He quotes an eyewitness, Majid Nawaz, now a prominent figure in Hizb ut-Tahrir:

> ... the boy, a Christian student of Nigerian extraction, had been throwing his weight around and being generally offensive towards Muslims and about their attitudes. Someone had phoned Saeed [Nur], who, as he had done previously, turned up within fifteen minutes. The pair confronted each other outside. The black boy drew a knife.
>
> Saeed remained calm, looked the boy in the eye and said, 'Put that knife away or I will have to kill you'.
>
> The boy did not respond. Perhaps he thought Saeed was bluffing. Saeed walked closer and warned him again. Exactly what happened next is unclear, but within seconds Saeed had pulled out Abdul Jabbar [a dagger] and thrust it into the boy's chest.

Husain called the killing the direct result of Hizb ut-Tahrir's ideas.

Just over a year later, when the murder went to court, the *Guardian*'s brief summary ran under the headline, 'News In Brief: Asians Deny Murder Charge'. It began: 'A dispute over a game of table tennis led to a group of Asians murdering a Nigerian student.'

Four men were accused of killing Obanubi. One of those found guilty was not a student or Asian, but a regular college visitor, Saeed Nur. Nur was an African Muslim of Somali origin. He carried a card that said 'Soldier of Allah'. During Nur's murder trial, a number of witnesses identified him as having engaged in vigorous pro-Muslim activity in the run-up to Obanubi's murder, which had included threatening the Nigerian. Reporting of Nur's sentence was banned because jurors could not decide on a verdict for one of his co-accused and it went for retrial. One man had been acquitted outright – Kazi Nurur Rahman.

The retrial took more than six months to return to the Old Bailey and ended in an acquittal. But by this time the story seemed clearer. *The Times* headlined a short account, 'Muslims "Killed Student Over an Insult to Islam"'.

In retrospect, this gang murder was a jihadi milestone. For Ed Husain, one of the Islamist extremists at Newham that day, it began a long journey away from violence towards a very different interpretation of Islam. For Kazi Rahman it led to Pakistan and, a few years later, to an appearance on my programme, *Five News*.

In 2001, at a shabby house in Lahore that served as the Pakistan office of Bakri's Al Muhajiroun, Hassan Butt wheeled out a rather nervous and masked British Muslim to talk to Five reporter Jon Gilbert. The man told British television viewers: 'I cannot wait for the day that I meet British soldiers on the battlefield and see them run ... I am very happy to kill them.' The nervous young man was Kazi

Rahman, and thankfully he never got an opportunity to make good on his threats.

One of Rahman's associates in that Lahore office was Mohammed Junaid Babar, an American supporter of Al Muhajiroun. He too was interviewed by Gilbert condemning his country. That soundbite, rebroadcast on CNN, brought Babar to the attention of the FBI. Three years later, in April 2004, they arrested him in New York.

Babar's plea-bargaining deal with the FBI included an agreement to testify against a Canadian, Mohammad Momin Khawaja (who had been arrested on 29 March 2004) and a number of British men who had been arrested the following day.

Some of those men were the fertiliser bomb gang, under the leadership of Omar Khyam, who were storing ammonium nitrate for use in possible terrorist attacks. (During their surveillance operation the police swapped it for cat litter.) Khyam and his associates had come to light during Operation Crevice, a surveillance operation initially centred on a Luton taxi driver who was allegedly in contact with a senior al-Qaeda figure in Iraq (and now detained at Guantánamo).

The Crevice surveillance operation also turned up two of the men who, fifteen months later, would go on to carry out suicide attacks on the London underground system – Mohammed Sidique Khan and Shehzad Tanweer. In March 2004, their names were placed on a list of 40 'desirables'. It focused attention on Rahman too. He was placed on a list of fifteen 'essentials'.

We know this from an anonymous briefing after Omar Khyam and his gang were found guilty of their plot. On 30 April 2007, the Associated Press reported on the Khyam group's links with the 7/7 bombers, which had been kept secret for two years in order not to prejudice their trial:

A government security official, who briefed reporters on the case in exchange for anonymity, said fifteen other terror suspects were ranked as higher priorities than [Mohammed Sidique] Khan and [Shehzad] Tanweer.

Only one of those terror suspects ended up going to jail: Kazi Rahman. Babar had told the FBI that Rahman had once planted an arms cache near a university in Lahore and later offered it for use to another of the Operation Crevice targets.

Despite these claims and his presence on MI5's 'essentials' list, no action was taken against Rahman until a fortnight after the 7/7 bombings. So how exactly did Rahman wind up going to prison?

▮ Entrapment? ▮

On 20 July 2005, MI5 launched the first phase of an entrapment operation aimed at putting Rahman behind bars. He was introduced – it's unclear by whom – to a security service officer. Together, they discussed counterfeit money, passports and the possibility of weapons purchases.

At some time shortly after this meeting, Rahman appears to have flown to Bangladesh. It didn't come up at his guilty plea, but a Bangladeshi news agency reported a curious incident on 8 August 2005. Six Muslim passengers were taken off the British Airways flight from Dhaka to London.

The airport's head of security told the agency that they had to check some passengers at British Airways' request. The airline, he said, had been told by British Intelligence that someone travelling in a wheelchair could be a suspected criminal. The passenger was a woman. One of her two male companions was identified as Kazi Nurur Rahman. Security officials also detained three Moroccans. The plane was searched but nothing was found and the six off-loaded passengers went on to London on a later flight. The incident was headlined as no more than a security scare.

Still, it's hard not to believe that this story – discoverable via an internet search – would have compromised Rahman in the eyes of any terrorist associates. At the very least, it would have alerted Rahman and others to the fact that his movements were being tracked by the British security services.

Despite this, a little over two weeks later, Rahman and the MI5 agent met again. He indicated that he could set up a meeting with an arms dealer. Phone calls were exchanged. Another meeting took place in a café at Liverpool Street Station on 29 September and the meeting with the 'arms dealer' Mohammed – actually an undercover police officer – was fixed for 4 October at South Mimms service station on the M25. Rahman asked Mohammed for three Uzis with silencers and 3,000 rounds of ammunition. A week later, Rahman met once more with his original contact.

The next meeting with Mohammed was on 15 October, again at South Mimms. Rahman handed over £2,000 (later rather bizarrely found to be £3,000). Rahman discussed the possibility of acquiring rocket-propelled grenades and surface-to-air missiles. On 19 October, Mohammed texted Rahman with a price for these weapon systems. What happened next?

Rahman flew to Saudi Arabia. It's not clear why a major terrorist suspect in such a case was allowed to leave the country, nor with whom he met and how he was monitored while he was away. He returned to Britain on 10 November. A week later, on 17 November, Mohammed and Rahman met again. When asked about the details of the weapons exchange, Rahman said he would bring someone along to check their authenticity.

The weapons handover was scheduled for 11 a.m. on Tuesday 29 November with the initial meeting at South Mimms services, off the M25. Rahman hadn't managed to find anyone to bring along with him. Mohammed introduced him to another undercover officer, Iqbal. Rahman drove with him to a backstreet in Welham Green where he was shown three Uzis. After seeing them, he expressed concern that he was being set up in a sting and went back to his car to call Mohammed. It was at this point that Kazi Nurur Rahman was arrested by armed police.

The strange thing about the entrapment is that you could equally read Rahman's involvement as an attempt to sting his suitors. When he asked for advanced weapons systems, the astonishing £70,000 price-tag under discussion would have made him the best-financed terrorist in British history. Previously, he mistakenly handed over £3,000 instead of £2,000 – who gave him that money?

Now comes the interesting part. Before he entered his guilty plea Rahman claimed to have been an MI5 informant. It's worth considering exactly what he told police on 1 December 2005. This is from the court documents:

> [Rahman] said that he was not a terrorist and had no link with terrorist organisations, claiming that he had been acting under duress, fearing for the safety of himself and his family. He further claimed to have been tasked by an Anti-Terrorist Organisation, which he claimed to be in fear of.
>
> An interview then followed at 1:38 p.m. in which he gave a story stating that he had been specifically tasked to infiltrate terrorist groups. He claimed that he was recruited when he was on remand in prison about ten years before [for the Obanubi killing] and that he had been involved in a number of successful operations. He referred to meeting his handlers in hotel rooms and that he had been paid tens of thousands of pounds over the years. He later stated that he had no knowledge of the fact that there were Uzi machine guns in the van and that he had expected to see two or three handguns and that he was to report back to his handlers by text message ...
>
> In a later interview when disclosure had been given con-

cerning items found at the search of his home address, Rahman stated items seized by police would have been planted by the Anti-Terrorist Organisation. He identified this organisation as being MI5.

On 2 December in a further interview concerning 55 Huddlestone Road, he stated the following:

> I have come to the conclusion that 55 Huddlestone Road is owned by either MI5 or you guys and I have been badly stitched up.

He then referred to a map of Afghanistan inside the premises and stated that it should be examined for fingerprints, stating that either police or MI5 fingerprints would be found on it.

Rahman subsequently retracted these claims and was sentenced to nine years' imprisonment. It was only after the Crevice trial finished in May 2007 that reporting restrictions on Rahman's case were finally lifted. It didn't generate much coverage. Attention focused on the potential for Rahman to purchase the surface-to-air missiles he'd expressed an interest in, and the conjecture that they would have been used to bring down an airliner. The headlines?

- Maniac Planned Missile Hit on Jet – *Daily Express*

- Plumber 'Planned to Bring Down Jet' in Rocket Attack – *The Times*

- Passenger Jet Terror Plot Foiled After 7/7 – Press Association

▮ Informants, information and public credibility ▮

So what do we make of the delayed reporting of Rahman's guilty plea and conviction?

On the one hand, thanks to the security services, an individual who fantasised about committing terrorist acts was not given the instruments to realise those fantasies.

On the other, recalling the tenacity of police in pursuing every contact of David Copeland's, we might ask why the entrapment operation was so long in coming against Rahman and why similar stings were not launched against the other 'essentials' listed with him? We might be concerned about the management of informants, their role as agents provocateurs and the safety of entrapment operations. We might also be concerned about the management of terrorist threats with the involvement of foreign agencies for whom the safety of UK citizens is a lower priority and with their own *raisons d'état*.

Informant-handling is a murky business. It came up in the Northern Ireland Police Ombudsman's report on the killing of Raymond McCord Jnr. The report looked at management of informants in the province during the 1990s. Nuala O'Loan found that over a number of years police acted in such a way as to protect informants from being fully accountable to the law.

Ironically, an inquiry like O'Loan's could not take place now, since Special Branch responsibilities in terrorism were moved to MI5. (A window of accountability closes before it half-opens.)

In October 2003 the Police Service of Northern Ireland (PSNI) carried out a major review of all their informants, as well as informants who were run by the military with the knowledge of PSNI. It was carried out by the Covert Human Intelligence Source Risk Analysis Group (CRAG for short). As a result, nearly a quarter of all police informants had their relationships ended. Half were 'retired' because they no longer had access to relevant intelligence. The remaining 12 per cent were 'let go' because the CRAG review found that they had been too deeply involved in criminal activity for their continued employment to meet the legal and ethical standards set by Parliament. That means 12 per cent of informants were found to be involved in criminal activity. That percentage is actually misleading, since what we really want to know is the scale and nature of that criminal involvement.

Management of informants wasn't put on a statutory basis until the Regulation of Investigatory Powers Act in 2000. That required record-keeping and reviews of covert human intelligence sources, but not necessarily of casual contacts. It also appointed an Intelligence Services Commissioner to review the authorisation of informants – currently a retired Appeal Court judge, Sir Peter Gibson.

In his April 2007 speech, then National Coordinator of Terrorist Investigations, Peter Clarke, called for greater public understanding of the terrorist threat. He criticised the length of time taken to bring cases to court. He criticised too the reporting restrictions imposed because of evidence emerging in one case prejudicing jurors in another. Clarke said:

> I just wonder if we could be bolder and, dare I say it, trust juries to distinguish the prejudicial from the probative … Is it not important for government, business, community leaders and the wider public to be able to consider, in an informed way, what the impact of … an attack would be if it had actually happened? Should we not be considering the political and economic consequences, or the potentially devastating impact on community cohesion? Apart from anything else, I honestly believe that the public are entitled to know why airport security is becoming ever more intrusive and inconvenient.

At the time, media attention was directed to his criticism of leaked information about arrests in an alleged plot to kidnap and behead a British Muslim soldier. His call for a change in our rules on contempt went largely unreported.

That call was echoed by the Lord Chancellor and the Attorney General.

In November 2006, the Director of Public Prosecutions publicly backed the decision to allow reporting of the case of Dhiran Barot after he pleaded guilty, while seven co-accused were awaiting trial, in a step towards recognising that juries can make decisions on the evidence presented to them in court.

Barot was jailed for 40 years in 2006, reduced on appeal to 30. Clarke described the case like this:

> It is no exaggeration to say that at the time of the arrest there was not one shred of admissible evidence against Barot. The arrest was perfectly lawful – there were more than sufficient grounds, but in terms of evidence to put before a court, there was nothing. There then began the race against time to retrieve evidence from the mass of computers and other IT equipment that we seized. It was only at the very end of the permitted period of detention that sufficient evidence was found to justify charges.

Clarke and others in law enforcement wanted reporting of the case to inform or influence the debate on pre-trial detention. It wasn't that successful. Melanie Phillips wrote of the Barot case in the *Spectator*:

> ... the case attracted relatively little media attention. Certainly, the lurid details of the plot were fully reported, but there has been virtually no analysis of the significance of the Barot case. There's been no discussion of what it tells us about the sheer scale of the threat to this country, or how best we should protect ourselves against it.

On the other hand, in June 2006, 'security sources' told the *Sunday Telegraph* that a possible Sarin attack on the London Underground had been foiled with the arrest of two brothers in Forest Gate. Peter Clarke told reporters: 'This operation was planned in response to specific intelligence.'

More than a week after the Forest Gate arrests, Phillips wrote in the *Daily Mail*:

> That affair is now cloaked in rumour and counter-rumour. Some police officers are reported still to believe that there is a chemical weapon somewhere, even if it was not where they thought it was. Another report says that before the raid Scotland Yard had serious doubts about the credibility of the MI5 source. Yet another says the original tip-off did not come from an MI5 informer, but from someone who phoned the Met's anti-terrorist hotline.

However, in April 2007, Peter Clarke once more publicly declared that such a raid would not have been launched without very good reason.

We're already familiar with the murder acquittal where the police announce that they're not looking for anyone else. So, who to believe?

▌ Improving public understanding ▐

One of the great barriers to public understanding, not just in terrorist trials but in all criminal proceedings, is the wider impact of that activity on our society. The legal proceedings in the case of Tundi Obanubi effectively shut down wider discussion of the impact of Islamist recruitment on campuses. So too did the pronouncements of the police. Politicians, the press and the public were denied the opportunity to debate how to respond to a threat by a security agency seeking to manage that threat for them.

Our tradition of public communication – in our courts and in our parliament – is adversarial. We would do well to remember that tradition when it comes to enabling public understanding of the issues arising out of terrorist activity. We can't guarantee understanding, but without allowing political, partisan discussion of those issues (and allowing juries to make up their minds on the facts and evidence presented to them in court), we risk the slow process of justice blinding us to the rapid transformations taking place around us.

The other problem we face is the lack of public communication by the security services themselves. This makes the default position of reporting the 'security source'. These sources are likely to be at best, disinterested public servants, at worst, apologists or blame-shifters. Their claims are almost impossible to verify.

Let me illustrate that with an example, a stretching of the thin existing facts to reach one of those fantasy conclusions so beloved of conspiracy theorists.

Recall that we have an official, but anonymous, confirmation that Rahman was one of the fifteen 'essential' targets identified by MI5 after March 2004. Our conspiracy theorist would point out that no action was taken against him until late July 2005. And that none of the remaining fourteen people on that list had been arrested at the time of the statement in April.

The conspiracy theorist would also point to two of the 7/7 bombers who were on the list of 40 desirables. One of them was Mohammed Sidique Khan, the supposed ringleader of the 7/7 conspiracy. He was recorded in Omar Khyam's car. Here's some of that recording from the *Daily Telegraph*, although it appeared in many places:

> At one point, Sidique Khan asked Khyam: Are you really a terrorist?
>
> KHYAM: They are working with us.
>
> SIDIQUE KHAN: You are serious, you are basically?
>
> KHYAM: I am not a terrorist, they are working through us.
>
> SIDIQUE KHAN: Who are? There is no one higher than you.

It's a strange fragment of a conversation.

A conspiracy theorist might put that together with the timing of the move against Rahman and ask: What if the security services had been double-crossed by someone that they had previously relied on as an informant? They might then wonder if the security services didn't decide to rapidly terminate any existing arrangements on the grounds that – well, you couldn't be too careful.

So, was Rahman a casual contact of the security services? Someone whose services had not been properly dispensed with? Or was he a jihadi opportunist just waiting for a chance?

Just to puncture the speculative bubble, remember Rahman pleaded guilty. And he withdrew his claims about MI5.

But does what you've learned about his history inspire you with confidence that this is the totality of his story? Do the anonymous sources and leaks satisfy your citizen's curiosity that intelligence efforts are being handled in a way that gives you confidence?

By contrast, the Copeland case is not a fertile breeding ground for conspiracy theories and rumours. It does not lurk at the back of the public imagination, poisoning the image of the police and security services as secretive, homophobic or racist. I would argue that's because the trial and the facts presented to the public denied them the ability to flourish.

▮▮ The future ▮▮

I don't really think we can expect reporting as it is currently resourced to provide either the answers or the kind of public scrutiny these important questions require. (I don't even know if we can ask the public en masse to be interested.) And there are few incentives for journalism to shoulder the burden of informing the public in the first instance (although there are niche opportunities for that to happen). So what can we do?

Publicly accountable communication might restore our confidence. The pressure of open, public communication is as much about the burden it places on an organisation to tell a consistent story, as it is about the communication itself.

We need public access to trial records, information and documents. The current system in which provision of trial transcripts is farmed out to agencies is impossible to justify. To find out what went on in the Central Criminal Court in 2007 cost £1.37 per 72 words. An hour of court time cost £120–130 to transcribe. You might wonder just how open this made justice?

Court transcripts and documents ought to be made publicly available online. It is bizarre in the extreme that Old Bailey records from the 17th to 19th centuries are freely available and searchable on the internet, that the Hutton Inquiry transcripts and documents are posted online, but not the cases coming before our most important criminal court every day. In a modern information society, their non-availability is actually an abuse of the public's trust.

This surely needs addressing as part of a wider review of the public provision of information. Once that material is freely available, let journalists do what they are good at – market it, scrutinise it, argue over it, examine it. And let interested parties and the general public do the same online.

I'm sure the security services would not want to rely on the vagaries of news planners and assignment desks to ensure that information on their successes went duly noted. I'm sure too that the public and Parliament would feel the same about information on their failures.

We need more effective institutional oversight of the security services. In the United States, the Office of the Inspector General in the Justice Department has played an important part in auditing the FBI's performance as it shifts from law enforcement to terrorism prevention. Our own domestic security service, which is now called on to play a similar role to the FBI, needs at least the same degree of regular, organised scrutiny.

In the US, several Congressional committees exercise oversight in respect of the FBI and its operations. Here, it is just one – the Intelligence Select Committee. The Prime Minister, with Opposition consultation, appoints its members. Ideally, the House of Commons should elect that committee. More committees, where appropriate, need to be able to scrutinise MI5 operations to ensure that security policy really is 'joined up.'

The final issue that needs addressing is libel. Some individuals have won large settlements from news organisations after being wrongly identified as terrorist suspects. Being a suspect is not the same as being found guilty in a court of law. The suspects in the killing of Stephen Lawrence were publicly identified by the *Daily Mail*. They have never been found guilty of his murder and yet live under the shadow of suspicion. Would a jury be minded to award them libel damages? We will all have to get used to a society where a presumption of innocence is replaced by an absence of legal conviction. It's a realistic consequence of developments like control orders and of the data trails we leave behind us in everything we do.

None of this will prevent the international conflicts of interest that arise in countering a global terrorist threat, but it might give us confidence in the probity and effectiveness of our own nation's part in that effort.

▮▮ Conclusion ▮▮

Yes, it all comes back to public information. And it matters even if you think the public aren't rocket scientists. In fact an example from the world of rocket science (okay, recoverable manned space flight) probably best sums up the importance of public information.

Physicist and Nobel laureate Richard Feynman was asked to help investigate the disaster which destroyed the space shuttle Challenger in 1986.

Feynman explained with piercing clarity the way in which NASA had let its safety standards slip to meet tight launch schedules, while all the time convincing itself at the very highest level that nothing was wrong. Feynman concluded his elegant and eminently understandable account of what went wrong like this:

> Let us make recommendations to ensure that NASA officials deal in a world of reality in understanding technological weaknesses and imperfections well enough to be actively trying to eliminate them.
>
> They must live in reality in comparing the costs and utility of the Shuttle to other methods of entering space. And they must be realistic in making contracts, in estimating costs, and the difficulty of the projects. Only realistic flight schedules should be proposed, schedules that have a reasonable chance of being met.
>
> If in this way the government would not support them, then so be it. NASA owes it to the citizens from whom it asks support to be frank, honest, and informative, so that these citizens can make the wisest decisions for the use of their limited resources.

Frank, honest and informative. That's a start. I hope that throughout this book it's possible to see that it's not the media but rather ourselves we shouldn't trust.

We're trapped in the language of relationships and a mess of statistics attempting to make sense of something that is positively ancient – our need as social animals for stories to trade and as rational beings for hard information.

The media can never solve that puzzle, because we can't

solve it. However, there are important things we can do to make sure that we aren't lied to.

First and foremost, we need to remind ourselves of the limits of the media in providing us with important information. Those boundaries can't be reshaped by some moral revolution, they need to be recognised. Where important information falls outside the media's retreating boundaries, we need to think of new ways to keep it available, so that we can access it and act upon it.

New psychological research is emphasising again how pivotal bad information is in shaping our opinions.

The brain has a rule, say the psychologists: if it remembers something well, it is likely to be accepted as truth. The more we hear things (right or wrong, true or false), the better we remember them. In the battle for information, this places a premium on repeating things that are wrong.

However, the power of the media to misinform has to be set against the potentially repressive regulation required to impose 'the truth', and the force that the powerful resort to most often to control the public – silence.

Let's tread warily.

Index

Liddle, Rod 42–3
Lindbergh, Charles 158–61
Lipset, Seymour Martin 148
Liverpool Street Station 197
Lloyd George, David 127, 132
Lloyd, Sir Nicholas 121
London Lite 100
London Paper 100
London Underground 195, 202
Long Island 158
Los Angeles Times 84
Louisiana 105
Louisville 70, 157
Louisville Herald 91
Luce, Henry 164–5
Lynch, Jessica 35

MacKenzie, Kelvin 121
Madrid 164
Mafia 136
Mail on Sunday 111
Major, John 120–3, 192
Malcolm and Barbara: Love's Farewell 28
Manchester United 147
Manhattan 158
Mani Pulite 134–5
Mao, Chairman 120
Marathon, Operation 190
Marbut, Robert 141–2, 165
Markets for Information Goods 54
Marsh, Kevin 43–4
Marx, Karl 120
Mather, Samuel 175
Matthew, Gospel of *see* Gospels
McAlpine, Lord 121
McCann, Gerry and Kate 106
McCann, Madeleine 96–7, 106, 156
McCarthy, Pam 70
McCord Jnr, Raymond 200
McLean, Bethany 186
media
  and market dynamics 96
  and politicians 122, 130–5, 137
  and the Bible 168–82
  and Tony Blair 119–120
  and trust 15, 20, 30, 35–6, 94, 141,
    146, 153, 185, 208
  barons 17, 20, 110–14, 117, 132,
    155, 127–30, 133
  business of 51, 56, 115–17, 21, 24–6,
    43, 106
  credibility 19
  cynicism 19, 29, 123, 148
  definition of 49–50
  dominates our lives 67
  establishment 20, 37–8
  failure to educate 81
  free 61, 104
  industry 20
  language of 39, 47, 87, 121
  limits of 138, 153, 209
  mainstream 79
  management of 118
  misinformation 123, 127, 132, 139,
    153, 181, 209
  monetises our time 51
  old 67
  power 118, 122, 127, 133–4, 139, 152
  regulation of 20, 106
  role of 183
  standards 17
Media Circuses 155, 158
Mediaset *see also* Berlusconi, Silvio
  137–8
Mentana, Enrico 134, 137–9
Merz, Charles 101
Meyer, Philip 150–1
MI5 *see also* British Intelligence *and*
  security services 196–207
Miami 155
Middle East, the 61, 95
Middletown 164
Miller, Gregory 184–5
Miller, 'Skeets' 157, 162
Milwaukee 155
Minneapolis 155
Mohammed, Omar Bakri 192
Morgan, Piers 180
Moscow 143, 164
Moses 108
Murdoch, Rupert 51, 110–15
  and Alastair Campbell 125
  and Fox News 58, 60
  and John Major 123
  and News Corp. 110, 113
  and Sky 114
  and the *London Paper* 100
  and the *New York Times* 113
  and the *Sun* 112, 113
  and Tony Blair 126
  influence of 117, 126–7
Murdoch: The Decline of an Empire 113
Murdoch: The Great Escape 113
Murrow, Edward R. 52–3
Muslims *see also* Islam 192–4
MySpace 110

Nabokov, Vera 69
Name That Tune 52
NASA 59, 208